THE LITTLE
BOOK OF
FOSTER
CARE
WISDOM

FAMILIUS

FAMILIUS

Published by Familius LLC, www.familius.com
Familius books are available at special discounts for bulk purchases,
whether for sales promotions or for family or corporate use. For
more information, contact Familius Sales at 559-876-2170 or email
orders@familius.com.

Library of Congress Cataloging-in-Publication Data
2018966234

Print ISBN 9781641701242
Ebook ISBN 9781641701730
Printed in China

Edited by Kaylee Mason
Cover design by David Miles
Book design by inlinebooks

10 9 8 7 6 5 4 3 2 1
First Edition

THE LITTLE BOOK OF

FOSTER CARE WISDOM

365 DAYS OF INSPIRATION
AND ENCOURAGEMENT
FOR FOSTER CARE FAMILIES

DR. JOHN DEGARMO

To little Bella, whom we love and miss.

CONTENTS

As I reflect on my seven years in foster care, there are some memories that rest in the forefront of my mind. The first is that I was adopted by my last set of foster parents— two very wonderful individuals who really wanted to give me a new beginning and provide me with a safe, well-structured, and loving home. I came into their home when I was only two years of age, and they were the only mom and dad I had ever known. Both of them were blue-collar and believed that hard work was essential to success in life. I admired both of them for instilling me with a strong work ethic growing up. Another thing that I remember was that my parents were what some people would call "old school." My father, Marion, was born in 1918, and my mother, Mary, was born in 1930.

Though both of my parents did the very best they could with what they had, they lacked the skills necessary to connect with me on an emotional level. Both had suffered various types of trauma within their own lives and believed that you just had to deal with whatever life threw your way. My father served as a marine in World War II and believed that men should not show emotions—he felt it displayed weakness. My mother suffered a chemical imbalance in her brain that caused her to be verbally and physically abusive at times.

Another event that I remember was failing the third grade and being placed into special education. This was 1977 and being a special education student was not the most popular thing to be. I'm not sure why that year was so emotionally challenging or why I found it extremely difficult to do my schoolwork. As I reflect on it now, I personally believe that if I had been given emotional support from my parents at home, I would have been an amazing student. I remember wanting so badly for my parents to support me and tell me that they were proud of me. However, those words never came. There is a term that's called "the self-fulfilling prophecy," which says that if you tell a child they are nothing long enough, they start to believe you. The same is true if you deposit positive words into the mind of a child.

Unfortunately for me, I was not given a lot of praise, and thus developed very low self-esteem and believed that my existence was a mistake. I felt alone, weird, sad, and totally out of place in my family. I remember wondering why my biological mother gave me up for adoption and why my adopted mother was verbally and physically abusive. I was confused as to why my adopted dad never told me he loved me and why he never took me to baseball games or played catch with me in the backyard. As crazy as it seems, I felt like they did not care and that I was a burden on them. Despite all of the things I felt and experienced as an eight-year-old boy, my life was forever changed when I met my third-grade special education teacher, Ms. Ritchie. Some people believe that angels live among us. Well I know firsthand that they do, because Ms. Ritchie was my angel.

Her presence was simply amazing and life changing. She instilled in me a thirst for life that still positively affects me to this day. I was not a very good student and would get frustrated when it came to my academic success because I felt like a failure. I felt like I was a stupid kid that nobody wanted. One day I was doing math and could not figure out the problem. I quickly became frustrated, broke my pencil, and began to cry uncontrollably. Ms. Ritchie walked over and asked me why I was crying. I told her that I was stupid and that I should give up trying because I would never get it right. At that moment, she got down on one knee and said three words that forever changed my life. She looked into my tear-filled eyes with so much love and simply said: Mark Anthony, YOU ARE SIGNIFICANT. The power of her words forever changed my life. That day she made a deposit into my emotional bank account, and as a result, I was shaped into the man I am today. I learned from that experience that the power of words can truly be transformational. I never imagined that one person could have such an impact on my life. One heart can truly make a difference.

If you are currently a foster parent, or are thinking about becoming one, just know that you are appreciated and needed in a massive way. There are thousands of children that need loving, safe, and stable homes. Being a foster parent is one of the most rewarding professions on the planet. It can also be extremely frustrating and arduous at times. However, you need not worry because within this outstanding book created by Dr. DeGarmo, you will find a plethora of practical tips and strategies designed to equip you with the necessary survival skills to become the greatest foster parent you can be. Having known Dr. DeGarmo for many years, I can say without question that his love for children and the child welfare profession is simply inspiring. He believes that *every* foster child has unlimited potential and is worth saving. If you read this book in its entirety, you will not only find survival tips, you will find the motivation necessary to keep pushing forward during difficult times. Most of all, you will gain a better understanding of what is necessary to inspire the foster kids you serve and to help them walk into their destiny and live a life filled with PURPOSE, PASSION, and unforgettable PRESENCE.

MARK ANTHONY GARRETT
Speaker, Author, Innovator
TeachersAreHeroes.com

PREFACE

I wasn't really ready to be a foster parent.

Sure, I went through the months of foster parent training and took the training courses. I had the background checks and home inspections. In addition, I had been a teacher for over a dozen years and had been working with children from all backgrounds each day. Oh, and need I mention that I was also a parent of three children, myself? To be sure, I thought I knew it all and that foster parenting would not pose too much of a problem for me.

Boy was I wrong.

Within twenty minutes of our first placement coming to live in our home, I recognized that I was not ready for foster parenting. The little four-year-old girl and her six-month-old sister were placed in our home late one evening, just a few weeks after our training had concluded. These two special little girls quickly taught me that—despite all my training, my experience as a teacher, and my years as a parent to my own children—foster parenting brought with it a whole set of unique challenges. I soon found out that I had a lot to learn.

Months later, when these two little ones left our family and were reunited with their grandparents, I recognized that I was not prepared for that transition, either. I was not prepared for the waves of grief and feelings of loss that washed over me. I was not prepared for the first of many heartbreaks I have since had as a foster parent.

As I travel the nation and globe working with foster parents, I often hear that so many had the same experience as I did—their training just did not prepare them for the day-to-day realities that only foster parents experience. In truth, so many foster parents are not ready for the challenges that come with caring for children in foster care. These foster parents that I speak to continue to cry out for help and ask for tips and strategies to help them care for children in need.

This little book you have in your hands is unlike any other I have written. I wanted to share with you, fellow foster parents, the very best tips and strategies for caring for foster children in your home and welcoming those children who have suffered so much into your family. This little book also contains something each day that I feel is of the utmost importance: words of inspiration.

I must be honest with you. There have been days that I have felt like I could no longer continue as a foster parent. There have been moments when I have been exhausted—both emotionally and physically. During those times, I have often turned to words of hope, of comfort, and of inspiration. I wanted to share some of these with you each day.

Let there be no mistake: foster parenting is a difficult job. Your life as a foster parent is unlike anything else you will ever do. Your friends and family members will not truly understand or appreciate what you do. You might even question if what you are doing is making a difference. Here's the truth about that: My friend, what you are doing is so important, so very important. What you are doing is life changing. You see, each child that comes through your home and is a part of your family is changed for the better. You are changing the world, one child's world at a time. It is my hope that you continue caring for children in foster care. There are so many children in care, yet so few willing to help. May the following tips and quotes aide you during your struggles and triumphs.

DR. JOHN DEGARMO
The Foster Care Institute

JANUARY 1

TIP #1: Don't rush into being a foster parent. Instead, take time to consider how it will change and impact you, your family, and your lifestyle. This is not a decision that should be made quickly. Take the time to gather the information you need to make this important decision.

> When you care for children in foster care and bring them into your homes and families, you help change their lives. Yet, your lives are changed, as well.
>
> **—JOHN DEGARMO**

TIP #2: When considering becoming a foster parent, contact your state child welfare system and learn what restrictions might prevent you from becoming a foster parent.

> As a foster parent, you have the opportunity to help children in need. When you foster a child, not only do you invest in their future and well-being, you change their life.
>
> **— JOHN DEGARMO**

TIP #3: Talk with your spouse or partner before seriously considering becoming a foster parent. Both of you must agree about children in need moving into your home and becoming a member of your family.

> Make sure that you and your spouse are on the same page with your parenting, and ensure that the two of you are consistent when it comes to all decision making with your foster child. Make your marriage the cornerstone of your home, and work to make it a productive and happy one.
>
> **— JOHN DEGARMO**

TIP #4: It is important to recognize that your marriage will change in some way while you care for children in foster care in your home.

> Children are educated by what the grown-up is and not by his talk.
>
> — CARL JUNG

TIP #5: When thinking about becoming a foster parent, talk to your own children about this important decision. Allow them to be a part of the decision-making process. Encourage them to voice any concerns they might have and listen to them with an open mind and heart.

> My biological children are a very important part of my foster parenting. Without them, my wife and I would not have been able to foster the forty-plus children that have come through our home.
>
> — JOHN DEGARMO

TIP #6: Recognize that having children from foster care living in your home will affect your own children. Make no mistake, the effect on your children can be wonderful, but it can be difficult at times, as well. It will be important that you prepare your children beforehand.

> Most importantly, though, my own biological and adoptive children have come to love their siblings from foster care and treat them as part of our own family.
>
> — JOHN DEGARMO

TIP #7: Now might not be the right time. Even if you and your family believe that you want to be a foster family, it is necessary to recognize if the timing is right or not. It might not be—and that's okay. Perhaps your family needs to wait a while.

> It is time for parents to teach young people early on that in diversity there is beauty and there is strength.
>
> —MAYA ANGELOU

TIP #8: Be prepared to accept that your own friends and family members may not approve of you becoming a foster parent or understand why you choose to do so. Some may not be supportive, while others may simply question your choice.

> My family, work mates, close friends, those at my church; all will discover what foster care is all about and what good parenting is about, just by watching what I do each and every day.
>
> **— JOHN DEGARMO**

TIP #9: Having a foster child in your house can be draining—emotionally, mentally, and physically. In order to have a child placed in your home, each member of your family must be in good mental and physical health. This includes no drug or alcohol abuse. You, and each member of your household, will have to pass a medical examination and provide a physical report from your doctor that will be turned into the child welfare agency and kept on file. Be prepared for this.

> Today. Today is the day we can help a child. Today is the day we can bring hope to a child in need. Today is the day that we can help a child start over again. Today is that day.
>
> — JOHN DEGARMO

TIP #10: Ask yourself these questions before beginning the process of becoming a foster parent: Do you have the patience required to be a foster parent? Are you prepared to say goodbye to a child that may have lived with your family for some time? Can you work alongside the birth parents of the child—even if they have committed horrible acts against the child?

> Children are apt to live up to what you believe of them.
>
> **— LADY BIRD JOHNSON**

TIP #11: Understand that you will have to work with a foster care system that is not perfect. You may become frustrated at times at how the foster care system works and need to be patient, open minded, and ready for challenging decisions you might not agree with.

> There have been moments when I have questioned whether or not I was making a difference. There have been times when I have grown frustrated with the system and have had to stand by and watch some of the children in my home go back to environments and situations that I knew were not healthy or safe.
>
> **— JOHN DEGARMO**

TIP #12: Recognize that you will have to work with and abide by the decisions of a court system and a judge and that you might not agree with the decisions made. It is important to understand that you are not in charge of many of the decisions.

> Frustration, although quite painful at times, is a very positive and essential part of success.
>
> — ROBERT BENNETT

TIP #13: You will, most likely, be asked to attend many meetings as a foster parent. Meetings with doctors, therapists, teachers, counselors, caseworkers, and perhaps even birth parents and biological family members of the children placed into foster care. Consider how this schedule of meetings might affect your own life, job, and family.

I am like a mamma bear fighting for her cubs;
I fight for my foster children with all that I have.
They are my children, and I will fight with all I have
in order to make sure that they are safe, that they
have all they need, and that they are loved.

— JOHN DEGARMO

TIP #14: Talk to other foster parents, through social media sites or locally, about their experiences, and gain information, strategies, and wisdom from them. No one truly understands or appreciates what being a foster parent is like better than another foster parent. They can give you insight into what you might expect when you become a foster parent to a child in need.

A baby is born with a need to be loved — and never outgrows it.

— FRANK A. CLARK

TIP #15: Think about the ages and genders of the children you would like to care for in your home. Consider what age and gender fits best into your family.

> When a child from foster care comes into my family and into my home, they become a part of my family and an important part of my home.
>
> —JOHN DEGARMO

TIP #16: Know what type of foster parenting you want to do. Do you want to provide short-term or long-term care? Do you want to be a respite home that cares for children in foster care while their foster family takes a break? How many children can you care for at one time? These are important questions to consider before becoming a foster parent.

When you hold your baby in your arms the first time and you think of all the things you can say and do to influence him, it's a tremendous responsibility. What you do with him can influence not only him, but everyone he meets and not for a day or a month or a year but for time and eternity.

— ROSE KENNEDY

TIP #17: Are you able to care for children with special needs—mental or physical? You should be able to answer this question before you sign up to become a foster parent.

> Each child is loved with as much love and compassion as I can possibly give.
>
> —JOHN DEGARMO

TIP #18: Understand that foster care is not adoption. While it is possible to adopt a child from foster care, most of the time the child will be placed into your home for a short time before being reunited with his birth parents.

> The opioid epidemic is the main reason for the alarming rise of children in foster care.
>
> — JOHN DEGARMO

TIP #19: It is okay to say "no." Embrace this tip today. There may be times as a foster parent when you simply cannot provide the resources and care that a child needs. There may also be times when you and your family don't think that the placement is the best fit. Other times, you may simply be overwhelmed. As a foster parent, you have permission to say "no" when you need to.

> Even as kids reach adolescence, they need more than ever for us to watch over them. Adolescence is not about letting go. It's about hanging on during a very bumpy ride.
>
> — RON TAFFEL

TIP #20: Be adaptable and be flexible. The life of a foster parent is often one of surprises, twists, and challenges. A strong foster parent is one that understands the need to expect the unexpected at any time.

> We care for these children because we DO care. Is it easy? Not always.
>
> —JOHN DEGARMO

TIP #21: When you feel that you are ready to become a foster parent, contact your local foster care agency or child welfare office. Some states have private foster care agencies, while other states only have state operated agencies. Determine which type of fostering best fits you, and then sign up for foster parenting classes.

> These children need someone to care for them and provide stability. These children need someone to love them.
>
> — JOHN DEGARMO

TIP #22: Be open minded. As you take your foster parenting classes, understand that there will be new ways of thinking about how to be a parent. Be open minded to new parenting ideas and skills. Do not fall into the trap that you know all about parenting. When you care for children in foster care, many of the new skills and ways of thinking you learn in foster parenting classes are necessary.

> Don't worry that children never listen to you; worry that they are always watching you.
>
> — ROBERT FULGHUM

TIP #23: Ask questions. The old saying that "knowledge is power" is quite true when it comes to foster parenting. The more you know about caring for a child placed into foster care, the better prepared you are to help meet her needs and demands. During your foster parenting classes, do not be afraid to ask the instructor questions if you are unsure about something.

> Sometimes, we may not be able to save a child from horrible and tragic experiences before they come to live with us. Yet, we are given the chance, as foster parents, to save them from experiencing other future horrors and to take them away from dangerous situations.
>
> — JOHN DEGARMO

TIP #24: Meet your new good friends. No one understands a foster parent like another foster parent, and you will find it helpful—and healthy—to have relationships with fellow foster parents. During your training sessions and classes, introduce yourself to others and befriend them. They are on this journey, just like you, to become a parent to a child in foster care. They have similar questions and concerns, and you will learn to lean upon them as you care for children in your home.

> For your friends and family, for your workmates and fellow church members, and for those in your neighborhood and in your city you are likely the only example of what a foster parent really is.
>
> —JOHN DEGARMO

TIP #25: Learn to be a team player. As a foster parent, you will need to work with others. These people may include the child's caseworker, a judge, birth parents and biological family members of the child, a Court Appointed Special Advocate (CASA), trained therapists, counselors, and teachers. When you work together in a professional and polite manner, you are not only building a positive working relationship, but you are helping the child in your home.

> You can learn many things from children. How much patience you have, for instance.
>
> — FRANKLIN P. JONES

TIP #26: Take time to learn about the paperwork. As a foster parent, there will be paperwork. Your local agency will set a per diem rate according to your foster child's age. A per diem rate is the daily amount of money you will receive in order to properly care for your child. Rates for children are broken down into three age groups: birth to five, six to twelve, and thirteen to eighteen. You will also have to document how much you spend on diapers, clothing, and other items.

> I have said it many times, in many places: foster parenting is the hardest thing I have ever done. It IS hard work. At the same time, it is also Heart Work. It is the most important job I have done, as well.
>
> — JOHN DEGARMO

TIP #27: Make sure your house is ready. You are responsible for providing a safe and healthy home environment for your foster child. Your home must be one that offers a feeling of security as well as one that is welcoming to your new foster child. Try to create an environment that is clean, tidy, warm, welcoming, and loving.

> Cleaning your house while your kids are still growing is like shoveling the sidewalk before it stops snowing.
>
> — PHYLLIS DILLER

TIP #28: Have a checklist of things to do or items to acquire before your foster child arrives. Here is what you might have on your checklist, depending on your foster child's age and needs:

- Alarm clock
- Extra seat at kitchen table
- Baby crib and mattress
- Fire extinguisher on every floor/level
- Baby bottles
- Kitchen cleaning items out of reach
- Bed made with extra blanket
- Light fixtures working properly in all rooms
- Brush and hair comb
- Medicine out of reach
- Car seat
- Mirror installed on bedroom wall
- Closet space and extra hangers
- Night lights in bedroom and nearby bathroom
- Diapers and baby wipes
- Soap, shampoo, conditioner, and toilet paper
- Dresser or cabinet for clothes
- Toothpaste and toothbrush
- Electrical outlets covered up
- Towel
- Exposed wires taken care of

In time of test, family is best.

— BURMESE PROVERB

TIP #29: Be ready for a call to come at any time. When a child is placed into foster care, there is often an immediate need for a home. That immediate need can come at any time, and you might get a call morning, noon, or night. Be prepared for your life and family dynamic to change at a moment's notice, and have baby supplies, school supplies, and a room ready for when that phone call comes.

I have learned to love each child that comes into my home in an unconditional manner and without reservations.

— JOHN DEGARMO

JANUARY 30

TIP #30: Be ready to adjust. The addition of a foster child to your home is sure to bring changes to your family dynamics and many adjustments will have to be made. After all, it is not just the adults in your home who will be fostering this child. Your own children will have an important role to play in the well-being and safety of your new arrival. Relatives may also be counted on to contribute to your foster child. You may also find that neighbors, friends, and church members wish to help you and your foster child. Keep all of these people in mind as you go through the adjustment period.

> Call it a clan, call it a network, call it a tribe, call it a family: whatever you call it, whoever you are, you need one.
>
> — JANE HOWARD

TIP #31: Perhaps the most important thing you can do to prepare for the arrival of a foster child is to educate yourself with as much background information and history as you can about the child. Ask those questions! Do not be concerned if you have many questions for your caseworker when you are first approached about placing a child in your home. While the caseworker may not have all the answers, you will find valuable information by asking.

> Every child deserves to have "Happy Birthday" sung to him. Every child deserves to have a birthday party in his honor. Every child deserves the chance to blow out candles on his day.
>
> —JOHN DEGARMO

TIP #32: Have a list of questions ready for when you get a phone call about placing a child into your home. Place a copy of your list on your refrigerator, in your wallet or purse, and in places where you can have it ready when the phone call comes. Your list of questions might look like this:

- How old is the child?
- Is this the first time the child has been in foster care?
- Why is the child in care?
- Are the child's medical shots up to date? Are there any medical concerns?
- Will the child need day care supervision?
- Is the child from the same town? Does the child need to be enrolled in your local school system?
- Does the child have any learning disabilities or special needs of any kind?
- Does the child have clothes? Will you need to buy diapers and baby wipes?
- Does the child have any anger management or extreme emotional issues that you need to be aware of?

So many children in our nation are without strong male role models. There are so many children in our country with absent fathers. It's time to change that. It's time for our churches, schools, politicians, and our society to begin taking a stronger stand on this issue. It's time that we all begin to encourage the fathers in our nation to take their roles responsibly. It's time we reclaim our children's fathers and daddies.

—JOHN DEGARMO

TIP #33: Recognize that not every placement is the perfect fit for your home and family.

There is a good chance that in the future the foster child we cared for may not remember our names. There is a good chance that in the future the foster child we cared for may not remember our faces. But many children in foster care who come through our homes will remember one thing: that for a period in their life they were loved. And some day down the road they will blossom into something better because of it.

— JOHN DEGARMO

TIP #34: Take some time to sit down with your children and remind them why you chose to be a foster parent. When the time comes, share with them the information they need to know about your new foster child. If they are too young to understand why a child might be in foster care, do not burden or confuse them with this information—they will simply not need details. Your older children, however, may be curious as to why the foster child is coming to live with them. Share with them what you know and remind them that the foster child is probably hurting and scared.

Foster parenting has created a sense of urgency within me to make a difference in the lives of those in need.

— JOHN DEGARMO

TIP #35: Your own children may have concerns. Perhaps they will be worried that they will have to share you with their new foster sibling or will resent that there is a new person joining their family. Ask them to share their feelings with you and listen to what they have to say. Reassure your own children that you will always be there for them.

I now am able to see the pain and suffering in others and am better equipped to help them.

— JOHN DEGARMO

TIP #36: Understand that the child placed in your home is likely not going to be the one you expect or imagine. Your first experience will probably not be a sweet little child who rushes into your waiting arms, laughing delightfully. Your foster child will likely be scared, frightened, and full of anxiety. He may have left his family moments ago, and have been just recently told that you are his family for the time being. Without a doubt, your foster child will be full of questions and swirling emotions.

> My children are the reason I laugh, smile, and want to get up every morning.
>
> — GENA LEE NOLIN

TIP #37: Each child that is placed with you will be different. Some may come to you with a head full of lice, while others might be covered in dirt and carrying the few possessions they own in a black plastic bag. In fact, they may only have the clothes on their back. Others may arrive clean and healthy with a suitcase full of clothing, a box of possessions, and some money in their wallet. What is important is that you do not judge your foster child based on arrival and appearance.

> You have made a difference. You have made a tremendous difference in the life of a child in need.
>
> — JOHN DEGARMO

TIP #38: The first impression you create with your foster child is often vitally important to how the following few days and weeks will transpire. Although it is impossible to predict how they will react when they first meet you, it is important that you approach this time with caution and care.

> One can never say "I love you" to a child enough times. They need to and deserve to hear it several times a day. "I love you" reminds children that they are valuable, that they matter, and that someone truly cares for them.
>
> — JOHN DEGARMO

TIP #39: When the caseworker pulls into your driveway with your foster child, go out to the car and welcome them—if possible. Introduce yourself immediately, with a warm smile and soft voice. Inform your foster child who you are and the role you will now play in their life. He or she may not understand the foster care system or what foster parents do. Additionally, do not insist that your new child calls you mom or dad. In fact, it is wise that you never insist upon this; the word "mom" may refer to the person who beat them, or the word "dad" may refer to the person who left their family. Allow your foster child to call you by your first name, if you feel comfortable with this, or by whatever name they are comfortable calling you.

> Loving a child doesn't mean giving in to all his whims; to love him is to bring out the best in him, to teach him to love what is difficult.
>
> — NADIA BOULANGER

TIP #40: As you help your foster child inside with their possessions, take them by the hand if they are a little one, or place a soft hand on their shoulder if they are a teenager. Actions like these can be reassuring and communicate that all will be okay, and that your home is a safe and caring place. Do not insist on hugging, as they may be too embarrassed or hurt to do so. After all introductions to the entire family have been made, take them on a tour of your house—their new home. Show them where they will sleep and where their clothes will be kept.

> It is especially important for us, as foster parents, to take all opportunities to communicate that we love the child in our home, and to do so in a variety of ways.
>
> — JOHN DEGARMO

TIP #41: After you give your new foster child a tour of your home, have a plate of hot homemade chocolate cookies and a glass of milk ready for them, if it is age appropriate. The smell of homemade cookies is very inviting—and everyone loves homemade cookies and milk. Ask if he or she is hungry and offer food. If they don't want any food, do not insist upon it. This is also a good time to sit down with the caseworker and fill out any necessary paperwork.

> Foster parenting has been a tremendous gift to me. And I bet it has been for you, as well.
>
> —JOHN DEGARMO

TIP #42: Have a nightlight already on in your foster child's new bedroom, if the room is dark. Have a nightlight on in the nearest bathroom, as well. Because it is a new house, your foster child might become confused in the middle of the night when looking for the bathroom. Additionally, make sure that your new child knows which bathroom to use.

Give light and people will find the way.

— ELLA BAKER

TIP #43: As your foster child adjusts to their new home and environment, they will require your extra time and patience, so give as much of it as you can. Remember, everything is new to them; there is a new home, new food, new "parents" and "brothers and sisters," and new rules and expectations. Perhaps even a new school, peers, and teachers if they move from another school system.

> You are planting a seed in the life of a child in foster care that WILL grow and WILL bloom. You may not see this transformation while the child is living in your home; this seed may not blossom until much later, but it will blossom if you plant it with love, water it with your tears, and nurture it with your time and compassion.
>
> — JOHN DEGARMO

TIP #44: Your new foster child may exhibit sudden outbursts of anger, aggression, sadness, or depression—or even telling imaginative stories about his or her birth family. They may even express no emotions at all. It is important that you do not take their behavior personally, as they are simply attempting to understand their feelings and cope the best way they can.

> There are so many children in care, yet so few willing to help.
>
> — JOHN DEGARMO

TIP #45: The new foster child in your home will be filled with questions; these questions stem from anxiety, fear, and confusion. How long will he remain in the foster home? When will he see his parents next? How often can he visit family members? These are questions that may weigh heavy on your child's mind. Make sure that you answer each question as honestly as you can. If you are unsure of an answer, let him know and reassure him that you will attempt to find out.

> Nothing you do for children is ever wasted. They seem not to notice us, hovering, averting our eyes, and they seldom offer thanks, but what we do for them is never wasted.
>
> — GARRISON KEILLOR

TIP #46: Building trust is essential for a stable family life, therefore building trust with your teen from foster care is an important step to her well-being. Give her space and allow her time to learn that she can trust you. Do not make promises that you are sure you cannot keep.

> Before I was a foster parent, I had some mixed views about the foster care system.
>
> — JOHN DEGARMO

TIP #47: It is likely that the child placed in your home has come from an environment where there were no rules, no expectations, and no consistency. As soon as possible, take some time to sit down with your new foster child and discuss the rules of your home, as well as your expectations. Listen to your foster child and encourage him to ask questions. It may be difficult at first, yet your consistency is essential. This is an important time for your family, as you begin to form a relationship with your foster child.

> What I have learned through my children is that they need more than just the check boxes designed by the system.
>
> — CONNIE GOING

TIP #48: Do not demand that a child follows your rules immediately. All families have some sort of routine and patterns of behavior that exist within their home. Depending upon the type of household your foster child came from, she may not be familiar with your day-to-day routine and may struggle to understand your rules. Because of this, she may test your rules.

> Children are not casual guests in our home. They have been loaned to us temporarily for the purpose of loving them and instilling a foundation of values on which their future lives will be built.
>
> —JAMES DOBSON

TIP #49: During the first few days of your foster child's placement into your home, spend time with him and try to get to know him; learn his likes and dislikes, his fears and concerns, and his hopes and dreams. You might be the first person who has ever taken time to listen to him. You may be the first person who tells him that they have potential and can succeed in life.

> Perhaps the greatest discovery my family and I are learning is that the amount of love one can hold in a heart never seems to end.
>
> — JOHN DEGARMO

TIP #50: Be an encouraging ear to your foster child and listen to her without making judgmental comments. Encourage her to express her feelings and emotions to you, but do not push the issue if she does not want to or does not feel comfortable doing so.

> Children are the world's most valuable resource and its best hope for the future.
>
> — JOHN F. KENNEDY

TIP #51: Your foster child's birth family matters to him. Allow him to discuss his birth parents and biological family members with you if he wishes to. Show interest and do not pass judgement in front of your foster child. As you allow your child to talk about his family, you are helping to build a relationship of trust between you and your child.

> Hugs can do great amounts of good — especially for children.
>
> — PRINCESS DIANA

TIP #52: If you notice that the child placed in your home has bruises or signs of physical abuse, report this to the caseworker immediately. Document the location of the abuse, a description of what it looks like, the time and date you first noticed it, and when you reported it.

Perhaps the biggest impact you can make with those children placed in foster care is to become an advocate of change.

— JOHN DEGARMO

TIP #53: A trained, professional counselor and therapist can be very helpful to both your foster child and your family. Do not be afraid to seek out a trained professional, or ask your caseworker about one, for the child placed in your home.

> There are a number of ways that faith-based organizations can create outreach ministries for children in foster care in your own area.
>
> — JOHN DEGARMO

TIP #54: When you awake your foster child the first morning after being placed into your home, gently encourage her to come and have breakfast. Your child may not remember where your kitchen is and may not know that she is allowed to eat. It is important to remember that many children in foster care do not have three meals a day, and therefore your foster child may not have eaten a breakfast in a long time.

> Eating habits are learned behaviors; they're not intuitive. So what your children learn to eat at home early in life sticks with them well into adulthood.
>
> —ANN COOPER AND LISA M. HOLMES

TIP #55: School may be the last place your child in foster care wants to go to after being placed into your home. He may have a very difficult time focusing on schoolwork and homework, as he may instead be focusing on survival and when he will see his family again. Do not expect your foster child to finish their homework those first few days. Instead, the emotional issues your child faces may take center stage.

> The outside world does not see the many challenges and struggles you may face on a daily, and sometimes hourly, basis.
>
> — JOHN DEGARMO

TIP #56: When a child is first placed into your home, clean or wash all of her belongings: clothing, shoes, jackets, bags, stuffed animals, toys, etc. It is likely that your child's belongings have not been washed in a long time, if ever, and they may carry germs or other unhealthy aspects with them.

> Ever since my foster parents came into my life, I knew that no matter what tomorrow brings, I can make it.
>
> — WHITNEY GILIARD

TIP #57: A warm bath or warm shower can go a long way in helping create a relaxing and welcoming environment for the child placed in your home. There is a good chance that the child has not had a bath or shower in some time. If age appropriate, allow your new foster child time to soak in a bubble bath or take a long hot shower. If it is an infant, a good bath can help not only keep the child clean but encourage it to play. A bath or shower can provide emotional benefits, as well.

> The child supplies the power but the parents have to do the steering.
>
> — BENJAMIN SPOCK

TIP #58: Be prepared to discover that water or bath time might be frightening to your foster child. You may never understand what triggers this fear, as it could come from an experience that occurred before coming to live with you. This fear may also come from the sudden change in your child's family routine and environment. If this is the case, try filling the tub with warm water and allow your foster child to play with some favorite toys outside of the bath before placing some special toys into the tub.

> Play keeps us vital and alive. It gives us an enthusiasm for life that is irreplaceable. Without it, life just doesn't taste good.
>
> — LUCIA CAPOCCHIONE

TIP #59: The first few nights are often very difficult for a child when first placed into a foster care home. For many children, bedtime is a reminder that they are not in their own home, in their own bed, and with their own family. Take time to reassure your child; read to him, sing a soft song, and get him a special stuffed animal for bed time. Find ways to make this scary time a little more comforting.

> You need to be your child's advocate. Your child is counting on you. Will you let her down?
>
> — JOHN DEGARMO

During my first few years of fostering, I was told repeatedly to "not take the teens." Everyone around me seemed to agree that I would "regret it." Luckily, my heart told me something else and I took in a sixteen-year-old pregnant girl, Kim, who was due in two weeks. Her water broke that night and for the following two years I had the great honor of fostering Kim and her son, Tyler. They were two of my very first foster kids. Kim came from poverty and a family of drug abusers. She only had a ninth-grade education and was approaching seventeen years old, so we decided that she should try to get her GED. She studied hard and refused to give up, while I pushed her and believed in her. It took her three tries, but she passed. It was because of Kim and Tyler that I went on to help more teen moms and their babies—and eventually to just teen girls. Nine years have passed, and I just saw Kim and Tyler for Tyler's ninth birthday. A strong bond still flows between them, and I am glad to still be a part of their lives so that I can witness it. On that day, I was able to hug Kim and whisper into her ear, "I am so very proud of you."

— GAY

TIP #60: Your new foster child may resist you and all that you have to offer. This is normal for a foster child. Remember, she may very well not want to be in your home, as it is not her own. You may even be perceived as the bad guy in the situation, thus you can't expect your foster child to embrace you and your family immediately—or even to like you. Be patient and understanding during this time.

> I have learned that raising children is the single most difficult thing in the world to do. It takes hard work, love, luck, and a lot of energy, and it is the most rewarding experience that you can ever have.
>
> — JANET RENO

TIP #61: There is a good chance that any rules and expectations you have for your foster child will not be met. This is especially true of the first few days and weeks. Instead of stressing about unmet expectations, use your time gaining trust and simply getting to know each other. It may take a while, but as a foster parent, you are in it for the long, tough haul.

> Don't think you are the only one, and don't give up. You can do this. I believe in you.
>
> —JOHN DEGARMO

TIP #62: It is also important to remember that foster children need structure, guidance, and consistency in all areas. This includes the setting of rules and expectations in your household. In order for your household to run smoothly, you must set some rules in place and let your foster children know what expectations you have of them.

It really does not get any easier when children move from your home and leave your family. But guess what? It shouldn't get any easier. This is how it really should be; these kids need you to hurt for them.

— JOHN DEGARMO

TIP #63: Be aware that your foster child may never have had rules of any kind in his home. He may not have had the responsibility of doing chores, and homework may be something completely foreign to him—as they may not have been expected or enforced. Additionally, manners may not have been taught or modeled in his family.

> The hardest job kids face today is learning good manners without seeing any.
>
> — FRED ASTAIRE

TIP #64: Personal hygiene may not have been established before your foster child came to live with you. In fact, you may be the first person to introduce this topic and conversation. Some may refuse to bathe or shower, while others may not want to put on deodorant, brush their teeth, comb their hair, or even wear clean clothes. Talk to your child about the importance of good hygiene. Be gentle and loving in this difficult conversation and remember that it will likely take time before you are able to change these lifelong habits.

> Children across the world are suffering from the hands of parents, from family, from adults, and from governments!
>
> — JOHN DEGARMO

TIP #65: You will need to ensure that your family's values and moral structure do not change as you care for a child from foster care. You probably do not accept violent behavior, disrespectful attitudes, profanity, or destruction of property within your home. Yet many foster children have not been brought up in this manner, and you may find that your foster child does not understand your values and morals.

> As you sip your morning coffee, there are children who are being abandoned by those who profess to love them.
>
> — JOHN DEGARMO

TIP #66: Work on the behaviors that you find most important first. When your foster child improves with one expectation, then it is time to begin focusing on another. All children enjoy praise from the adults in their lives.

> Your children need your presence more than your presents.
>
> — JESSE JACKSON

TIP #67: When you feel that the time is ready, sit down with your foster child and let her know your expectations. Be very specific, yet simple, in your explanation of your rules and expectations, ensuring that your foster child understands what you would like her to do and how she should behave. Make sure that your expectations are appropriate for her age as well as her ability level.

> The protection of a child often starts with you.
>
> — JOHN DEGARMO

TIP #68: When establishing rules in your household with your foster child, it is important that you stick to the rules already established. Foster children will shake up your household like nothing else will. Therefore, continuing to adhere to your normal rules will provide some consistency for your family members.

> Each time a child leaves, my wife and I experience a great sense of loss, even when we can be comforted with the knowledge that the children have gone to a good and safe home.
>
> — JOHN DEGARMO

TIP #69: You need to know where your foster child is at all times. Where is your foster child after school? Who is taking your foster child to day care? What is your foster child involved in outside of your home? Who are the adults in charge when your foster child is not in your presence? Is the child in a safe environment? Is the child in a positive environment? These are all questions that you need to focus on as a foster parent, as they will help to ensure that your foster child is in the most productive and safe environment possible.

> What feeling is so nice as a child's hand in yours? So small, so soft and warm, like a kitten huddling in the shelter of your clasp.
>
> — MARJORIE HOLMES

TIP #70: You will most likely have to correct your foster child's behavior while he is living in your home. It is necessary that you learn different approaches in regard to disciplinary methods, especially regarding children who have only known abuse. What works for one child may not work for another. Try rewarding good behavior, praising every success, time-out, time-in, natural consequences, and taking away privileges.

> There is a child out there, today, who needs a family, and who needs to be loved.
>
> —JOHN DEGARMO

TIP #71: There are times when we, as foster parents, need to "choose our battles," so to speak. We need to recognize that every battle does not need to be won and that every misbehavior doesn't need to be corrected. There are times when we need to look for win-win solutions that benefit both parent and foster child. We also need to understand that there are some house rules that can be flexible and some that must be maintained at all times for safety and well-being.

Adopting can be a welcomed and challenging path to building a family, and each situation is different.

— RACHEL GARLINGHOUSE

TIP #72: Time-outs may be old-fashioned, but they still work. Time-outs can be used when a child is having an outburst of anger, for aggressive behavior, or for open defiance. When used properly, placing your child in time-out allows her a few minutes alone and away from a distressing environment. Whether your time-out is having her stand in a corner, sit in a time-out chair, sit on the bottom step of a staircase, or go to another specific location, time-outs can be an effective way of helping calm a child when used correctly.

> The gain is not the having of children; it is the discovery of love and how to be loving.
>
> — POLLY BERRIEN BERENDS

TIP #73: Ideally, the length of time a child remains in time-out correlates with his age: one minute per child's age. For example, if the child is four years of age, the child might sit in the time-out chair for four minutes. If he is seven years old, he might stand in the corner for seven minutes. Keep this in mind when deciding discipline techniques.

> You NEED to ensure that you are taking care of yourself. Find the time you need for you and the help you need to care for not only the children in your home, but for yourself and your entire family. If you do not, all that you do will suffer.
>
> — JOHN DEGARMO

TIP #74: Ever heard of a time-in? Time-in works differently than time-out. Like time-out, time-in is a form of disciplining a child when issues of behavior occur. When a child is placed in time-in, the child is placed into close proximity to you, the parent. Time-in allows the child to be near you or another adult, instead of away, as in time-out. Don't be afraid to try a time-in as a form of discipline for your foster child.

> May you continue to love your foster child and may we all continue to comfort them as they experience the loss of their own family when they move to ours.
>
> — JOHN DEGARMO

TIP #75: Consider using a time-in. A time-in may look like one of the following examples:

- The child sits next to the parent on a couch or chair, while the parent reads a book to the child or the two of them listen to soothing music together.
- The child sits across a table from the parent and the two work on a puzzle together or play a game, while engaging in conversation.
- The child sits in a chair, stool, or even on a throw rug while the parent goes about doing daily household chores. Perhaps the parent is folding laundry in a bedroom, cooking dinner in the kitchen, or cleaning the lounge room.

> Parents need to fill a child's bucket of self-esteem so high that the rest of the world can't poke enough holes to drain it dry.
>
> — ALVIN PRICE

TIP #76: There are times when you might need to redirect a foster child's behavior. Redirection is a form of discipline that is becoming more popular in today's culture. Redirection allows a parent to guide and steer a child's misbehavior from one that is inappropriate to one that is more appropriate. When a child is redirected, it allows her to explore new opportunities, discover new experiences, and learn new skills.

> It's okay to say that foster parenting is hard.
>
> — JOHN DEGARMO

TIP #77: Don't be afraid to reward a child in your home. When a child is rewarded, he receives positive recognition for his efforts, behavior, successes, or achievements. Quite simply, when you reward a foster child in your home for his behavior and successes—no matter how small—you are reinforcing positive actions and encouraging him to do more of the same in the future. Perhaps this success is a good grade on a report card, helping with the dishes, going a day without telling a lie, or eating dinner without complaining; whatever the positive behavior or success, your child needs to know, from you, that you recognize and appreciate it.

Watching a four-year-old girl smile for the first time is healing for all.

—JOHN DEGARMO

TIP #78: When a child behaves in a way that is not acceptable in your home, one form of disciplinary action might be to take away or withhold a privilege. A privilege is something that we enjoy doing or having. For children, it might be staying up late on Friday nights to watch a movie, eating ice cream on Sundays, or going over to a friend's house. A privilege is different than a right. We all have the right to food, water, and shelter, but we don't have the right to eat our favorite box of sugary cereal or watch our favorite movie over and over again—these are privileges. When a privilege is taken away from a child as a form of discipline, it can help to reinforce that the negative behavior was unacceptable.

> Never say, "Oops." Always say, "Ah, interesting."
>
> — ANONYMOUS

TIP #79: If you are fostering a teen in your home, chances are likely that she may have experimented with drugs or alcohol. She may have also picked up the habit of smoking. As a foster parent, you cannot allow these habits in your home. You must be clear that they are not permitted and that there should be no smoking—either in the home or away from the home.

> A child who is allowed to be disrespectful to his parents will not have true respect for anyone.
>
> — BILLY GRAHAM

TIP #80: Let your foster teen know that he is not to have possession of matches, a lighter, or any form of tobacco or drug material at any time. Let him know what the consequences will be beforehand. If your foster child has already experimented with these prior to coming to your home, he might very well resist you strongly, resulting in confrontational moments between him and your family. Be prepared for this and remain consistent.

> There is a child in need, right now, who is in need of someone to say, "I care. I will take care of you. I will love you."
>
> — JOHN DEGARMO

TIP #81: It is not only important that you know where your foster child is at all times, it is essential. If your foster child should wish to visit a friend's house or another home, do a thorough check of who lives there, the environment she will be in, and the level of safety and supervision she will be under. Be sure to call the parents of the home your child wishes to visit; this will help to both ensure that the environment is a safe one and allow you to express any concerns you have about your foster child with them. If you feel that the friend's home environment is not a safe one, do not be afraid to say no to your foster child.

> Love and forgiveness are two actions that are intertwined and cannot be separated. If we truly are to love these children who come into our homes, then we need to forgive their family, as well.
>
> — JOHN DEGARMO

TIP #82: The supervision of your foster child is necessary in your own home, as well. It might be unwise to allow your foster child to play unattended, just as it might be with other children. If your child is in his room playing or even napping, make sure that his door is open, even if just a little bit. From time to time, check in on him and make certain that he is okay and not doing anything that you would disapprove of. If he is in the backyard, make sure that he will come to no harm from stray animals, sharp objects, unwelcome visitors, or simply wandering off alone.

> Life affords no greater responsibility, no greater privilege, than the raising of the next generation.
>
> — C. EVERETT KOOP

TIP #83: You may foster a child that has been sexually active in the past, due either to her own choices or the choices of others through sexual abuse. Perhaps the child is currently sexually active or was exposed to sexual behavior prior to her placement with you. Whatever the scenario, you must take extra diligence in protecting yourself from false allegations and possible accusations from the child.

> To be sure, our words have power, and our children need us to use these words in positive and healing ways.
>
> — JOHN DEGARMO

TIP #84: Whenever you are in the same room with a foster child who has sexually related problems, it is imperative that you have another adult in the room with you or, at the very least, within listening distance. This will not only protect you as a foster parent but will protect your child from making false accusations.

Remember, these children, despite the many forms of abuse they have been subjected to, still love their mommies and their daddies.

— JOHN DEGARMO

TIP #85: Know that you have limited time to make an impact in your foster child's life and to help them turn their life around. As the child will be placed in your home for a limited time frame, do not hold back in your care and love; foster your relationship with them immediately. Assume control, anticipate their behaviors, and when their behavior begins to turn negative, step in quickly with compassion, understanding, praise, and positive reinforcement.

> The unconditional love for your child, it's truly amazing.
>
> —JOURDAN DUNN

TIP #86: Learn to be not only an effective communicator, but the best communicator you can be. Use strong communication skills with the children in your home. Not only should you be an active and engaged listener, but you should be able to deliver clear messages in a friendly, comforting, yet parental tone of voice. When you communicate effectively, you are showing your child how to do so, as well.

> As a foster parent, it is important to remember that our foster child's biological parents are people in need, and they deserve our kindness and sympathy, not our anger.
>
> — JOHN DEGARMO

TIP #87: Build your foster child up. It is likely that the child placed in your home has never had anyone compliment or acknowledge their strengths. Do not focus on the negatives; instead, let your child know what their strengths are. Find something to praise them about each day. This will help them to heal, build a better opinion of themselves, and be empowered to try their best and succeed.

> The love of a family is life's greatest blessing.
>
> —ANONYMOUS

TIP #88: Not only should you build up your foster child's strengths, but you should accentuate the wonderful differences and diversity that lie within the child placed into your home. Build up their self-esteem and place positive focus on their cultural differences and racial identity.

> Everything we say or don't say makes an imprint on our child's heart.
>
> — PATTY HOUSER

TIP #89: Have a no-label family. The child placed in your home should be a member of your family. Do not introduce him or her to others as "a foster child." If you do, you are reinforcing to them that they may not be important enough or good enough to be in your family. Instead, introduce them as a member of your family.

Always look for opportunities to teach your foster child important lessons in love and humanity, and help them in their own path in life.

—JOHN DEGARMO

TIP #90: Many children placed into foster care come from an environment that was not a healthy one, diet wise. In fact, it is common for foster children to have no idea what good nutrition is. Show your foster child the importance of healthy eating habits by providing a nutritious diet and encouraging them to eat healthy snacks. Teach them why good nutrition is important.

> Sadly, not every child will receive it. Not every child will feel loved. Yet, every child deserves it.
>
> — JOHN DEGARMO

TIP #91: Being part of your family means helping out in the household duties. Find age appropriate chores that your foster child can do at home; this will give them a sense of responsibility, trust, and belonging.

What it's like to be a parent: it's one of the hardest things you'll ever do, but in exchange it teaches you the meaning of unconditional love.

— NICHOLAS SPARKS

TIP #92: If age appropriate, talk with the child from foster care in your home about sex—and be specific. For many of these children, your talk with them may be the first time they have had this discussion. If they have been sexually abused, they will need to have counseling, as well.

> While there are many forms of love, the strongest one, and most important for a foster child, is that of unconditional love.
>
> — JOHN DEGARMO

TIP #93: If you want to be the best foster parent you can be, you will need to work closely with your child's caseworker. Work to create a strong and healthy working relationship with the caseworker, as the two of you will be instrumental in helping your child get the help, resources, and services that they need.

Emotional difficulties such as a lack of self-worth, trust issues, and the need to be in control are often the result of a lack of unconditional and healthy parental love.

— JOHN DEGARMO

TIP #94: Take steps to develop lines of communication with your child's caseworker. Make sure both of you have current telephone numbers and email addresses for each other—for both home and work.

> We may not be able to prepare the future for our children, but we can at least prepare our children for the future.
>
> — FRANKLIN D. ROOSEVELT

TIP #95: Sharing information is essential. Make sure that you share all information about the child with your caseworker. Be honest about any concerns you might have in regards to the child and about any challenges you might have. Be open about the frustrations you might be feeling, as well. If you notice that your child is struggling to adjust to your home and family, express these concerns, also.

> All of me loves all of you.
>
> — ANONYMOUS

TIP #96: At some point, the child placed into your home may become sick. If he does, inform the child's caseworker as soon as you can, in both an email or other written form for documentation, and by phone. Even if it is for one day at home from a common cold or just not feeling well, you need to let your caseworker know. Caseworkers have the responsibility of documenting everything when it comes to the children on their caseload, including sickness.

> Perhaps the most important step you can take in helping your child from foster care is building trust with him.
>
> — JOHN DEGARMO

TIP #97: Before meeting with your caseworker, make sure that you are prepared. Have all the proper forms and information gathered together that you might need for the caseworker. This includes any school progress reports and report cards, teacher's names and contact information, medical paperwork, receipts and invoices, and other personal observations you may have noted about the child.

> To be in your children's memories tomorrow, you have to be in their lives today.
>
> — BARBARA JOHNSON

TIP #98: You may feel that your foster child's caseworker is not concerned with your child's needs when phone calls and emails are not answered right away. Remember, your child's caseworker may also be the caseworker for up to sixty other foster children. Time is something that caseworkers do not have in large amounts.

> Family makes the house a home.
>
> — ANONYMOUS

TIP #99: Your caseworker is going to want to talk with your foster child periodically. It is important that you give them privacy and space. Encourage your foster child to open up to the caseworker.

> Begin each day with a smile on your lips, love in your heart, and gratitude for the chance to share these with others.
>
> — JOHN DEGARMO

TIP #100: Not only do the caseworkers look after foster parents and foster children, they are responsible for working alongside the biological parents. Along with this, caseworkers have to ensure that all legalities with the child are taken care of, to have visitations with each child each month, to attend court hearings, and to deal with all of the paperwork. Remind yourself that burnout is common in child welfare careers and that your caseworker may need your help and understanding.

> There is no exercise better for the heart than reaching down and lifting people up.
>
> — JOHN HOLMES

TIP #101: Caseworkers have feelings, just as you do. They may disagree with a court's decision to have a child removed from your home, feel frustrated with how the system works sometimes, and have feelings of grief when a child suffers in any way. Remember that your caseworkers are human with human feelings, just like you, and they care for each child they are working with.

> No matter the age or ability of your foster child, they need you.
>
> — JOHN DEGARMO

TIP #102: Recognize that many marriages suffer during the foster process. When you are putting so much energy and time into your foster child, you may be so drained and exhausted that you neglect your spouse. Further complicating this, some foster children are skilled at pitting one parent against the other, possibly bringing heated and very unproductive arguments to your home.

> When you take a foster child into your home, you are making a commitment to "foster" that child.
>
> — JOHN DEGARMO

TIP #103: There will be times when you rely upon your spouse for help, strength, and decision making. Furthermore, if you have children of your own living with you, you will also need them to be supportive and on board with your decision to be a foster parent.

> Educate your children to self-control, to the habit of holding passion and prejudice and evil tendencies subject to an upright and reasoning will, and you have done much to abolish misery from their future and crimes from society.
>
> — BENJAMIN FRANKLIN

TIP #104: It is necessary that you spend some alone time with your spouse as often as possible. Perhaps schedule a date night once every two weeks or once a month. If you cannot do that, maybe eat lunch together, take a walk together in the neighborhood, or find another activity that allows the two of you to have some private time together.

"Foster" means to take care of, to help grow, and to help develop another person.

— JOHN DEGARMO

TIP #105: Movie time! Another way to spend time with your spouse is to close the bedroom door once a week, grab some snacks and food, and watch a movie in bed together.

> Your foster child may not express gratitude, return love, or show appreciation for what you are trying to do, but it is important to keep in mind that you are making a difference — a difference that could indeed last a lifetime.
>
> — JOHN DEGARMO

TIP #106: Do not forget about communication. Be open and honest with your spouse about your feelings and do not hide things from them. If something is bothering you, share this concern with your loved one. Additionally, when your spouse is sharing their concerns with you, be sure to listen; simply listen.

> We make a living by what we get, we make a life by what we give.
>
> — WINSTON CHURCHILL

TIP #107: When you are having an open and honest conversation with your spouse during your care for children in foster care, make sure that there are no distractions around. Turn off your TV, radio, computer, and phone and try to find a place where you will be uninterrupted by children. Perhaps even talk in your bedroom behind locked doors, if need be.

> Being part of a family means you are part of something special.
>
> —ANONYMOUS

TIP #108: When it comes to issues of child rearing, discipline, and other topics that relate to our foster parenting, it is necessary that you and your spouse agree as much as possible. Be willing to be flexible, overlook minor disagreements, and agree to agree on the major decisions as you care for children in need.

> Being part of a family is a reminder that you are loved and will always be loved.
>
> — ANONYMOUS

TIP #109: Some children in foster care know how to manipulate one foster parent more than the other. Remain united with your spouse, and make sure that you do not allow your child from foster care to come between you.

> The best way to find yourself is to lose yourself in the service of others.
>
> — MAHATMA GANDHI

TIP #110: When you care for children from foster care in your home, your own biological children may experience difficulties. They may have fears that "new brother or sister" will get all of the attention. Furthermore, they may feel that they are being "left out" by you and by the family.

> When will the rights of children become part of the Human Rights Movement?
>
> —JOHN DEGARMO

TIP #111: You may find that your own birth children test you and your household rules after your foster child arrives. Your birth children may be trying to see if there is consistency between how you treat them versus how you treat the child from foster care in your home, and if the same rules apply to everyone. They might even try to see if they can get away with new things due to time of upheaval.

HOPE is out there.

— ESTHER PILGRIM

TIP #112: Include ways for your own children to welcome their new foster siblings each time there is a new placement. Take your children shopping with you to purchase the new clothes, diapers, food, or other items you may need for the new child joining your family. Encourage your birth children to help arrange the bedroom for the new placement. Ask your biological children to create a "Welcome Home" sign.

> Parenthood...It's about guiding the next generation and forgiving the last.
>
> **— PETER KRAUSE**

TIP #113: Your birth children need time alone with you as their parent while you are caring for your foster children. Find ways to have this special time together. Read a book to them, go outside and play just with them, go for a walk, take them to a movie, or go have ice cream together.

It seems that as I grow older I become more and more appreciative and more grateful for all the blessings in my life.

—JOHN DEGARMO

TIP #114: It's okay for your own children to keep some things private and separate from their foster siblings. In fact, that's normal. Allow them to do so and help them find ways to. An example of this would be to have rules about privacy in bedrooms for everyone in the house.

> When a child is placed into my home, they become family the very first day.
>
> — JOHN DEGARMO

TIP #115: Introduce ways that all the children in your family can play and interact together. Watch family-friendly movies, encourage the kids to play sports, introduce board games, have a table in the house designated as the puzzle table where everyone can work on a puzzle, or take the children swimming. The list goes on and on.

> We don't stop playing because we grow old; we grow old because we stop playing.
>
> — GEORGE BERNARD SHAW

TIP #116: Create new family traditions in your home to build relationships between all in your family. Some traditions might be to start a Lifebook together for the children in foster care in your home, have family time or game night once a week, or celebrate the holidays in grand style and in your unique family way.

> My home is one that has been filled with more love than I could ever have imagined.
>
> — JOHN DEGARMO

TIP #117: Be a culturally aware and competent family. As the children from foster care are placed into your home, it is likely that they are culturally different from your family. Create understanding and awareness of other cultures, beliefs, and traditions in your home, as your own children may be unfamiliar with many cultural differences. Talk to them about possible differences and celebrate the differences in each child. This will help your children to develop strategies designed to combat racism and other cultural prejudices.

You call it chaos, we call it family.

—ANONYMOUS

TIP #118: Some of the cultural differences that children in foster care may bring to your home include race, gender, family history, political views, religious beliefs, appearance, family norms and values, and sexual orientation. Be prepared to discuss these differences with your biological children in an age appropriate fashion.

> The key to community is the acceptance — in fact the celebration of — our individual and cultural differences. It is also the key to world peace.
>
> — M. SCOTT PECK

TIP #119: Your own family and friends probably will not understand what you do as a foster parent, nor why you do it. Additionally, they probably will not understand or appreciate the different lifestyle that you lead as a foster parent. Do not take it personally. In truth, no one will understand your unique challenges and daily lifestyle like another foster parent.

A child's laughter is often healing for all involved.

— JOHN DEGARMO

TIP #120: While you have children from foster care in your home, your friends, family, and others may ask you questions like "which child belongs to you?" or "how much do you get paid?" Do not take offense to these questions; there is a general misunderstanding about foster care and foster parenting in our society. Instead, try to answer these questions as honestly as you can, while at the same time helping to dispel the myths with your answers.

> Some days, I just have to look at the mayhem around me and smile.
>
> — JOHN DEGARMO

We have always encouraged our children to erase the phrase "I can't do it" from their vocabulary. However, when my foster care journey began, I often found myself mulling over these exact words in my head. The crying, extra appointments, strain on our biological children, sleeplessness, and overall inconvenience that accompanied the first little one who was brought into our home was too much; the white towel of surrender was soon in my hand and ready to be tossed into the ring of foster care. Being a foster parent was too wearisome and overwhelming. That is, until I considered the truth: I can't do it alone. I had been trying to minister to my foster children and their families in my own strength, however I soon found out—point blank—that doing so only brings disaster. Now, the Lord is the one who gives me strength; while I am weak, he is strong. One of the many things he has given me is a community of support through his church. Our family is now surrounded with love, encouragement, practical help, and occasionally a great meal. The simple truth I have learned is this: Attempting to do foster care alone is akin to living on a deserted island. You can survive for a week, but soon enough you will become desperate enough to quit. Instead, ministering in God's strength and allowing his church to surround you will give you the support and stamina needed for this great task.

— TONY

MAY 1

TIP #121: Finding time for you will not be easy, but it is very essential. Make sure to do something you enjoy each day—and that you find relaxing in some way. Spend time with some friends, go for a walk, go out to lunch by yourself, read a book, or garden. Find a way to make time for you, as it helps to prevent exhaustion and burnout.

> Until you value yourself, you will not value your time. Until you value your time, you will not do anything with it.
>
> — M. SCOTT PECK

TIP #122: Foster parenting is a twenty-four hours a day, seven days a week job. There is very little time off. After a while, you may experience foster parent burnout. Burnout is a condition that happens slowly over time, which can make it even more difficult to recognize. In fact, many people do not recognize that they are becoming burned-out until they hit that wall, so to speak.

> As a foster parent, I find that I am constantly learning something new, on a daily basis.
>
> — JOHN DEGARMO

TIP #123: Burnout is often defined as exhaustion of physical or emotional strength or motivation usually because of prolonged stress or frustration. It can also be defined as fatigue, frustration, or apathy resulting from prolonged stress, overwork, or intense activity. For foster parents, these definitions can very much define their daily lifestyle, as they care for children who have significant emotional and physical needs.

I have experienced so many diverse and intense emotions through the years that my heart is flowing over with love for all.

— JOHN DEGARMO

TIP #124: One way to help treat burnout as you care for children in foster care is to recognize the signs. These signs may include forgetfulness, lack of sleep or insomnia, fatigue, anxiety, lack of appetite, chest pains or shortness of breath, dizziness or headaches, depression, anger, and apathy.

> An empty lantern provides no light. Self-care is the fuel that allows your light to shine brightly.
>
> — ANONYMOUS

TIP #125: A very real condition for foster parents and care givers is compassion fatigue, also known as Secondary Traumatic Stress, or STS. As a foster parent, you are often at risk of STS, as you not only work with children who have suffered trauma and anxiety, but you live with these children twenty-four hours a day. Dr. Charles Figley states that STS is "the natural consequent behaviors resulting from knowledge about a traumatizing event experienced by a significant other. It is the stress resulting from helping or wanting to help a traumatized or suffering person."

Anyone can be audaciously present in a youngster's life, thus creating an environment of hope and a legacy of love for those who desperately need both.

— KIM COMBES

TIP #126: One reason that you might suffer from compassion fatigue is that as you care for children who have suffered in some way, you also feel their pain and their suffering. You take it on yourself, upon your shoulders, and into your heart. You over-empathize with the situation at hand and in your home.

Time spent with family is worth every second.

— ANONYMOUS

TIP #127: Another reason you might suffer from compassion fatigue is that you may have experienced a traumatic event in your life or suffered from personal loss. When you care for others who have experienced similar trauma to your own, your own past experience might be re-triggered, making you more at risk for internalizing the trauma of the child you are looking after.

> If your compassion does not include yourself, it is incomplete.
>
> — JACK KORNFIELD

TIP #128: Finally, you might suffer from compassion fatigue due to lack of recovery time on your behalf. You may not have given yourself distance so that you could heal personally from your own grief and pain. Also, you may not give yourself "time off" from an emotionally, mentally, and physically demanding lifestyle. Already worn down, you then continue to listen to the horror stories your foster children have lived through, time and again, and it may only wear you down further.

> If you experience grief and loss when your foster child leaves, this is a reflection of the love that developed between you and your child; a reflection of the love that you gave a child in need.
>
> — JOHN DEGARMO

TIP #129: Finding time to heal and recover from burn-out and compassion fatigue means sometimes saying "no" to the next placement call. Make no mistake; it is okay to say "no" once in a while as a foster parent. You need to recognize that you need time for your family to recover and heal. You may need to take some time off in order to grieve the loss of a child from foster care from your home and from your life. The power of the word "no" allows you the important time away to recover and be a stronger foster parent for the next child.

> What I love most about my home is who I share it with.
>
> —ANONYMOUS

TIP #130: Stay in the moment. This may be difficult for you, but it is important to focus on the here and now, instead of what might happen or what could be. As you worry about what might happen in the future, you lose the chance to embrace and appreciate what is happening in the present. Indeed, as you allow your own concerns to overwhelm you regarding future events, you leave the moment behind and are unable to help in the present. You are unable to truly help and love the children in your home if you are overwhelmed with the things you have no control of.

> Accept yourself. Love yourself as you are. Your finest work, your best movements, your joy, peace, and healing comes when you love yourself. You give a great gift to the world when you do that. You give others permission to do the same: to love themselves. Revel in self-love. Roll in it. Bask in it as you would sunshine.
>
> — MELODIE BEATTIE

TIP #131: Allow your heart to break. There will be people who insist that you should not get too attached or emotionally involved with the children from foster care placed in your home. The opposite is true. It is indeed healthy for you to become emotionally invested and attached to the children living in your home and as part of your family. If you instead try not to become too attached in order to protect yourself, you will not be able to help the ones that you are trying to care for.

> We are choosing to take care of children that are not ours, and doing so in a selfless manner.
>
> — JOHN DEGARMO

TIP #132: Get out there and sweat! Study after study indicates that exercise goes a long way toward treating burnout and stress. Exercise is able to act as a sort of antidepressant medication, as it helps to alleviate moderate forms of depression. Furthermore, when you exercise regularly, it helps to prevent future burnout and gives you an opportunity for some personal quiet time.

> Not only do I talk with my children about the sadness they might be feeling, I allow them to see my own sadness. I allow them to see Daddy cry.
>
> — JOHN DEGARMO

TIP #133: What is your diet like? When you eat foods that lack nutritional value, or foods that are considered "junk food," it can lead to a lack of energy and even a crash in your own mood. Good dieticians will encourage you to reduce your sugar intake, eat a great and healthy breakfast, drink up to eight glasses of water a day, and follow a regular healthy diet.

> Many people think that discipline is the essence of parenting. But that isn't parenting. Parenting is not telling your child what to do when he or she misbehaves. Parenting is providing the conditions in which a child can realize his or her full human potential.
>
> — GORDON NEUFELD

TIP #134: Sleep can be difficult to find when you are a foster parent. You may have troubling finding a good night's sleep when you experience burnout or compassion fatigue, or you may sleep too much and cannot find the energy to get out of bed and face the day. Getting a good night's sleep is essential to your health, well-being, and productivity, as well as in helping treat burnout.

> I admit it freely. I can't do it by myself, and I don't have all the answers when it comes to foster parenting.
>
> — JOHN DEGARMO

TIP #135: Remain calm and be patient. When you lose your patience with a child, you lose control of the situation. Keep in mind that many children in foster care have never been in homes where issues are addressed in a calm and rational manner. Many of these children come from environments that are filled with anger and hostility. Your own loss of patience and control reinforces to them that this response is normal and acceptable. When a child in your home is trying your patience, as the saying goes, try to remain calm. Respond to your child in a calm fashion—and with compassion and patience. It will not only teach the child how to behave in the future, but will also help to lower your anxiety and stress level.

Family: Where love never ends.

— ANONYMOUS

TIP #136: Call your own time-out. When you struggle with remaining patient, it is okay to call your own time-out. If you feel that you are losing control of your own emotions, do not let your ego interfere or be afraid to ask your spouse or partner to step in and take over a situation. Let your child know that the two of you will talk at a later time—this can allow you both to cool off or calm down—and step outside or into another room. Then give yourself time to cool off.

> It's not selfish to love yourself, take care of yourself, and to make your happiness a priority. It's necessary.
>
> — MANDY HALE

TIP #137: Mother's Day can be a very hard day for children in foster care. Often times, more than anyone else, children in foster care miss their mothers. Mother's Day is a reminder that your foster child is not with his mother, but instead with strangers: his foster family. Schools, churches, advertisers, and society place great emphasis on Mother's Day with cards, flowers, gifts, and stories, but don't overlook that it can be a very emotionally stressful day for your foster child.

> To be sure, what I thought I knew about children in foster care, and about the foster care system, was as far from the truth as possible. Like most of the general public, I had false ideas and beliefs about foster children and much of it was negative, I am afraid to say.
>
> — JOHN DEGARMO

TIP #138: If your foster child has lived in multiple homes, Mother's Day can be even more difficult for her. She may have lived with several foster mothers and never formed a true attachment with a mother figure. As a result, Mother's Day may hold no significance for her.

> We live in such an amazing country, so it may be hard sometimes to realize, but the foster children in America are the orphans of this country.
>
> — JOSHUA THERRIEN

TIP #139: If your foster child is open to the idea, help him create a Mother's Day card for his mother. Perhaps order some flowers to be delivered to the birth mother's home with your foster child's name on it. Encourage your foster child to call his mother on this day. However, if he does not wish to do any of these, do not pressure him into it, as it may cause additional trauma and anxiety.

All that I am, or hope to be, I owe to my angel mother.

—ABRAHAM LINCOLN

TIP #140: Don't take anything too personally. When a foster child living in your home calls you names, pushes your buttons, disobeys you, or treats you poorly, it can be a challenge not to take it personally. Remember, though, the child is most likely not attacking you personally. She may be scared, hurting, afraid, and confused, and she may not know how to properly process her emotions and feelings, so she instead lashes out at you. Remind yourself that the negative behavior is not about you, but about your child's trauma. Then, do not respond emotionally and instead focus on the child's behavior—not her emotion.

> As foster parents, we are to help those children placed in our home to heal. We do it in a number of ways, yet love is at the core.
>
> —JOHN DEGARMO

TIP #141: Learn the art of compromise. Become someone who is flexible regarding a child that may argue and fight with you often. Learn when to "choose your battle." Recognize that you do not need to win every battle, and that every misbehavior by your child does not need to be corrected immediately. There are times when you need to look for "win-win" solutions for both you and your child.

> Having somewhere to go is home. Having someone to love is family. Having both is a blessing.
>
> —ANONYMOUS

TIP #142: Remember that every word you say to a child in need does indeed matter. Children in foster care need to hear words of kindness from you. Words of affirmation, patience, kindness, trust, and compassion are building blocks in a child's life and are essential to their well-being, mental health, and emotional stability.

> No act of kindness, no matter how small, is ever wasted.
>
> — AESOP

TIP #143: Placement disruption is the term used when a child is removed from a home and placed into the custody of a child welfare agency—and thus into a foster home. For many children, this is a frightening time, as fear of the unknown can quickly overwhelm a child. Other children are filled with anger, as they emotionally reject the idea of being separated from their family members. Feelings of guilt may also arise within the foster child, as the child may believe that he had something to do with his separation from his family. Still other children experience self-doubt, as they feel that they simply did not deserve to stay with their family. Be aware of this as you begin your journey as a foster parent.

> So many need us, as fellow human beings, to lend a helping hand.
>
> — JOHN DEGARMO

TIP #144: Issues from anxiety can manifest themselves in a number of ways. Perhaps the most common manifestation among foster children is separation anxiety, an excessive concern that is brought on by being separated from their home, family, and those to whom they are most attached. Indeed, the more a child is moved from home to home, from one foster placement to another, the bigger the concern becomes.

What can you do to promote world peace? Go home and love your family.

— MOTHER TERESA

TIP #145: One way you can protect yourself as a foster parent is by documenting everything that occurs in your home while you are caring for children in foster care. Documentation can help protect you from any questions regarding your children from foster care—from false accusations made against you, to concerns about how you respond to your foster children's needs.

> Whatever you would have your children become, strive to exhibit in your own lives and conversation.
>
> — LYDIA H. SIGOURNEY

TIP #146: You can document in any number of ways. You can use a journal, diary, or notebook of any kind. Documentation can also be in the form of a calendar or behavioral chart, and can be recorded on a computer, laptop, iPad, or tablet through email or word documents.

> I have learned to love deeper, more openly, and without abandon.
>
> — JOHN DEGARMO

TIP #147: Record and save any emails between you and your foster child's caseworker, teachers, counselors, doctors, therapists, or anyone else involved in the child's case. You can do this by setting up an electronic folder on your computer just for emails about the child. Print out a copy of each email, as well, and keep it in a folder.

> A person's a person, no matter how small.
>
> — DR. SEUSS

TIP #148: How you record and document your experiences with your child is important. Do not create a diary of your feelings and emotions concerning the child. Instead, simply record all that transpires in the house and with the child. Do not share your opinions on issues or about the child. Instead, observe what transpires with your child in their day-to-day life. Write in an unemotional and unbiased fashion, writing only about the facts of what happened.

> A family doesn't need to be perfect; it just needs to be united.
>
> — ANONYMOUS

TIP #149: You may want to have a personal diary for your own feelings and emotions as you care for your foster child. This is perfectly fine—even healthy. Simply do not include this journal as part of your official documentation.

> In family life, love is the oil that eases friction.
>
> —FRIEDRICH NIETZSCHE

TIP #150: Your documentation should begin the day your foster child arrives. Observe and record any conversations with the child's caseworker about the child's placement. Then record how your foster child was when she arrived in your home. How was she dressed? What possessions did she have with her when she arrived? What was her emotional state like upon arrival? How were her eating and sleeping habits? What kind of paperwork did she have with her when she arrived?

> The love in our family flows strong and deep, leaving us memories to treasure and keep.
>
> — ANONYMOUS

TIP #151: Document all daily progress and events in your home regarding your foster child. Record how he interacts on a daily basis with members of your family and document how he interacts with friends, neighbors, family members, and even pets.

For each child that has come through my home, I give thanks.

— JOHN DEGARMO

TIP #152: As you give praise and compliments to your child from foster care each day, document how she responds to these words of praise. Record how she helps around the house, any positive behavior that she displays, and any significant conversations the two of you have.

> Family isn't always blood. It's the people in your life who want you in theirs; the ones who accept you for who you are. The ones who would do anything to see you smile and who love you no matter what.
>
> — ANONYMOUS

TIP #153: If your foster child should display any negative behavior, make sure you document not only what happened, but when and where it occurred. Record the conversation you had about it and any consequences that might have occurred as a result. It is also important that you document how your foster child reacted to the consequences.

> You don't choose your family. They are God's gift to you, as you are to them.
>
> — DESOMOND TUTU

TIP #154: If your child from foster care is ever on any kind of medication, it is important that you fully document it. Record what type of medicine he is taking, what it is for, how much he takes, and how often he takes it. Record when he becomes sick, how he is treated, and any doctor appointments or visits. Also document if he missed any days of school and keep a copy of all doctor's notes regarding the child.

> For each child that spent time in the foster care system while living with my family; I shall always love you.
>
> — JOHN DEGARMO

TIP #155: Record and document any meetings you might have with your child's teachers, school counselors, or school administrators. If possible, ask if you can take notes during any meetings with these school employees and explain that it is simply for documentation reasons. Also keep copies of any progress reports, test grades and results, and any other paperwork the school gives you.

It's time for our churches, schools, politicians, and our society to take a stronger stand on caring for our children.

— JOHN DEGARMO

TIP #156: If your child from foster care should ever have an encounter with police or law officials, make sure that you document it completely. Record the reason that the encounter happened; the time, date, and location of the event; and how your foster child might have responded to the encounter. Keep copies of any paperwork that law officials give to you.

> The most precious jewel you will ever have around your neck are the arms of a children.
>
> — ANONYMOUS

TIP #157: Many children in foster care see a therapist or counselor on a regular basis—this is quite normal and can be very healthy and beneficial. These counselors and therapists are trained professionally and are experts in their field. Document any meeting or session that occurs between a trained professional and your foster child, including the time, date, location, and how the child responds afterward.

> Wheresoever you go, go with all your heart.
>
> — CONFUCIUS

TIP #158: Accidents happen and kids are going to be kids. If the foster child in your home should ever injure himself in any way, make sure that you fully document it. Even if it is something as simple as a bloody nose, a skinned knee, or a scratch on an elbow, it is important that you document it. Record how the injury happened, the time and location, and how you treated the injury.

> When a child from foster care is placed in my home, I want to know as much about the child as I possibly can.
>
> — JOHN DEGARMO

TIP #159: Don't forget to have a sense of humor. Laughter can be very healing and greatly reduce stress. A sense of humor is essential when trying to maintain emotional health. As a foster parent, you might find that you just need to "laugh off" those situations that bring you unwanted stress. Laughter indeed can be the best medicine.

> The more you become interested in them, and the more you show that their interests are important, the better they will feel about themselves, and their placement into your home.
>
> — JOHN DEGARMO

TIP #160: Try to find some sort of joy in your own life each day. As you lift up children in your home with words and acts of praise, remember to find joy in the life that is happening all around you. Find reasons to smile at work, while shopping, and at home. Children can sense when you are not happy and when you are stressed, and that can bring stress to them, as well.

> Yesterday is history. Tomorrow is a mystery. Today is a gift. That's why it is called the present.
>
> —ALICE MORSE EARLE

TIP #161: Teach your children in foster care how to cook. There is a good chance that no one has taught them how to cook anything at all. Cooking is a skill that they will surely need when they leave the foster care system, and one that will help them to prepare for adult life.

> One of the most important reminders for you, as a foster parent, is the fact that you need to take care of yourself physically, mentally, and emotionally.
>
> — JOHN DEGARMO

TIP #162: Be aware of the many benefits of teaching children how to cook. It can help build self-esteem and form healthy bonds between you and the child. Additionally, cooking teaches children important math, reading, and even chemistry skills. When learning to cook, children are often more willing to try new foods and healthier diets. Cooking is also a way to introduce a child to new cultures.

> Every day may not be good, but there is good in every day.
>
> —ANONYMOUS

TIP #163: Just like cooking, gardening can be of tremendous benefit to children in foster care. The simple act of planting a flower can be a joyous event and can help to bring healing to a child who has suffered. Go ahead and get your hands dirty in the soil with your foster child.

> Being a parent is a wonderful calling and a gift.
>
> — JOHN DEGARMO

TIP #164: Growing a garden can help a child to grow in many ways. Gardening will allow your child to spend time with you, to learn about good nutrition when gardening with fruits and vegetables, and to have more patience. At the same time, children often enjoy planting seeds and watching them grow. Along with that, gardening teaches children about the importance of environmental stewardship.

> Have a heart that never hardens, and a temper that never tires, and a touch that never hurts.
>
> — CHARLES DICKENS

TIP #165: Many children in foster care come from homes where they did not know where their next meal might come from. Sadly, so many of these children frequently go to bed hungry. When you teach a child how to grow food, you teach her how to provide for herself and help her avoid feelings of anxiety about not having the next meal.

Don't neglect who you are and what makes you special.

—JOHN DEGARMO

TIP #166: Be aware that you live in a different world and reality than your children in foster care do. This is especially true regarding online technology and social media. You may spend a lot of time in front of a computer or online device for your job and may enjoy social media as a way of entertainment and communication; online technology and social media is a world that you visit and perhaps live in during part of your day. For today's children, it is a world that they inhabit. The difference is significant.

One kind word can change someone's entire day.

— ANONYMOUS

TIP #167: Children in foster care often feel that they have no control over their lives. They have no control of being abused or neglected, have no control over being removed from their homes and families, and have no control over being placed into your home. They have no control over being placed into a new school or with any other aspect of their lives. The only feeling of control they might have is through online technology. Youth in foster care feel as if they can create and control their own online persona. It is important to be aware of this as you attempt to understand and discipline your foster children.

> It's okay to say that sometimes you just feel like no one understands what you are going through.
>
> — JOHN DEGARMO

TIP #168: Be aware that children in foster care are look-ing for love and acceptance and that they often go online and to social media for just that reason: to find someone to love them. Social media offers children in foster care a way to express how they truly feel and to share with oth-ers their hopes, dreams, and fears. Foster children often search for what they feel is missing in their lives, for someone to accept them for who they are, and for some-one to love them.

Be awesome today.

— ANONYMOUS

TIP #169: The foster child who is craving someone to pay attention to them, be their friend, and love them is easy prey, meaning they are easy targets for online predators. Sexual predators seek out their victims by "luring" them in, encouraging them to reveal personal details and information about not only themselves, but their family members as well. Online predators develop relationships with their victims slowly, known as "grooming," usually in an unthreatening way. Predators scour the internet through chat rooms and social network sites, looking for children who are technically more advanced than their parents. Building a relationship over a period of time—over the course of weeks and sometimes even months—child victims feel that they can trust their new "friend." It is important that you are aware of the dangers your foster child might stumble across.

> Don't hold back in love, give love with all your heart.
>
> — JOHN DEGARMO

TIP #170: How aware are you? Are you familiar with your child's online activities? Do you know what your foster child is watching and playing online? Do you know all the sites your foster child is visiting online? Do you know all the contacts your foster child is having conversations online with? Do you know who your foster child is reaching out to online, or who is reaching out to him? You must be vigilant and aware at all times.

Every child is an artist.

— PICASSO

TIP #171: Become involved in your child's life, interests, and activities—both online and offline. Know all of your child's contacts and people that your child talks with on-line. Make it a rule that your child cannot be a friend to anyone online that she does not know personally.

Be a voice, not an echo.

— ALBERT EINSTEIN

TIP #172: Be persistent in warning your foster children about dangerous and inappropriate sites. There are so many online sites that offer dangerous material, information, videos, games, and resources. Many children in foster care have never been warned about these dangers.

> May this be the year that more children find that family, find the forever family, they deserve.
>
> — JOHN DEGARMO

TIP #173: As you care for children in foster care in your home, you need to have all of their passwords and log in information for their online devices and social media accounts. This is not an invasion of their privacy. Instead, it is simply a way to protect the child. Without this information, it is impossible to see who is reaching out to your child, who is trying to harm your child, and what your child has access to.

> There needs to be less paperwork, less "red tape," and more action on behalf of the child.
>
> — JOHN DEGARMO

TIP #174: Closely monitor your child's online actions, as well as their cell phone for any disturbing messages, texts, and pictures—and let him know you will be doing so. Ensure that you have access to your foster child's online activities so that you can monitor what he is doing. Remember, you are not the child's friend, you are the parent; you need to take all measures available to protect the child and your family.

> People are eternal and made for community with one another.
>
> — JENN AND TJ MENN

TIP #175: Protective filters and browsers should be in place, helping to block your foster child from accessing harmful sites. Set up clear guidelines with your foster child about all online use, and post the guidelines near a computer as a consistent reminder.

> Real children are never perfect, and perfect children are never real.
>
> — ANONYMOUS

TIP #176: You are the instructor and have a great deal to teach the children in your home about online technology and social media. Teach your foster child not to believe everything that comes across a computer screen or online device. Also teach her to notify you of any site or contact that might be suspicious in nature.

> Climb ev'ry mountain, Ford ev'ry stream, Follow ev'ry rainbow, 'Til you find your dream.
>
> — RICHARD ROGERS

TIP #177: Keep credit card details somewhere safe where foster children cannot access them, and make sure not to save credit card details online. Make sure that 'click to buy' options are not activated. There are many sites that ask the user for credit card information, including online gaming sites, music sites, movie streamers, and other entertainment sites.

> Our caseworkers need to be given more time, more money, more resources, and more understanding from the public, from the courts, and from foster parents.
>
> — JOHN DEGARMO

TIP #178: Your child's birth parents and biological family members may try to reach out to your foster child at any time through social media and online technology. This form of communication is often unmonitored and unsupervised by you and the caseworker, as it can be done in secret. This type of online communication can be dangerous, as false accusations can be made and arrangements to meet can be set up—all without you or the caseworker knowing.

> A child we have given all of our unconditional love to has left our home, and the grief can be overwhelming at times.
>
> — JOHN DEGARMO

TIP #179: Today's form of bullying looks very different than it did in years past. Cyberbullying is a term you need to be familiar with as a foster parent. Cyberbullying is the platform that the twenty-first century bully uses to inflict pain and humiliation upon another; it is the use of technology to embarrass, threaten, tease, harass, or even target another person.

Be kind whenever possible. It is always possible.

— DALAI LAMA

TIP #180: It is very difficult to identify who a cyberbully is, as the bully could be anyone behind a computer or online device. One way to help protect your child from cyberbullying is by consistently monitoring your child's online devices. When you see that your child is being bullied online, contact your child's caseworker as well as the school the child attends, as the bully may be a student that attends the same school as your child from foster care.

It's the little things that make life wonderful.

— ANONYMOUS

TIP #181: Cyberbullies can follow their targeted victim wherever the child may go, simply using online technology and social networking sites. Whether the targeted victim is in school, at the park, at the movie theater, or at home, they can be bullied whenever they have a cell phone or access to online technology. This form of bullying is non-stop, as it can last twenty-four hours a day, seven days a week. It is a good idea to educate yourself about cyberbullying.

> We must be the change we want to see.
>
> — MAHATMA GANDHI

In the last two years, my family has welcomed seven children from foster care into our home. These children were born in my heart and I will forever be their mother. When a foster child first enters our home, we reach out to the family to ensure them that their child is safe, taken care of, and loved. All the while, we pray for both the child and the family; one thing I have learned as a foster parent is that foster care is not easy for anyone involved. There is heartache on all sides. Furthermore, it is crucial to recognize and respect your own heartache and implement self-care. Of course with the heartache also comes happiness. There is nothing like the joy you feel when you see your foster child smile because his family is ready to welcome him home. It is times like these when I feel both joy and heartache simultaneously. Luckily I have strived to form friendships with my foster children's families, and have been able to continue watching my former foster children grow. These small joys make all the stress, long nights, and heartache of foster parenting worthwhile. In fact, the growth that my family has experienced through foster care has been worth every tear. My advice is simply to enjoy every moment with your foster children—no matter how difficult they may be—because you never know what tomorrow may bring.

— MELANIE

TIP #182: Cyberbullying can be done through emails, chat rooms, social network sites, text messages, cell phones, and even websites. There are countless ways a child can be bullied with this type of technology, and the number of ways is increasing as technology continues to advance. Talk to your foster children about cyberbullying and let them know that they can always come talk to you if they feel bullied.

> As foster parents, we need to reshape the conversation, showing and educating all around us what foster parenting is truly like, what challenges the children face, and how others can help through a number of methods.
>
> — JOHN DEGARMO

TIP #183: Be aware that foster children in particular are easy targets for cyberbullies. Cyberbullies often seek out victims who are new to a school, thus children from foster care become easy targets. As foster children often move from home to home and school to school, it is relatively simple for a bully to spot a foster child.

> The time is always right to do what is right.
>
> — MARTIN LUTHER KING, JR.

TIP #184: Foster children with special needs are also targeted by bullies. Along with this—as many foster children appear to have low self-esteem due to the many emotional, physical, and psychological challenges they face—foster children are often helpless to protect themselves from bullying, in whatever form it may take. Cyberbullies also typically target children who are less popular in school. If your foster child falls under these categories, be prepared for how to handle cyberbullying.

> We are what we repeatedly do. Excellence, then, is not an act but a habit.
>
> — WILL DURANT

TIP #185: For many foster children, gossip about them spread through online venues is especially hurtful. Many are targeted by their peers through social networking sites simply because they are in foster care. By posting or sending cruel forms of gossip, cyberbullies not only bring immense emotional pain to their victim, they also damage the foster child's reputation and relationship with their family members, friends, and acquaintances. Be a source of love and kindness to your foster child if he ever experiences cyberbullying.

> Love is a language. Kindness is a language. Compassion is a language. What kind of language are you speaking to a child today?
>
> — ANONYMOUS

TIP #186: Sexting is the act of sending a sexual message or nude or semi-nude photo to another person over an online device. Be aware that for today's foster youth this is considered a normal part of everyday life. Indeed, it is the twenty-first century form of flirting, and a large percentage of today's youth have either received a sext message or have sent one.

> Want a solution to a drug-free world? Raise these kids in love! Want to raise an army of world changers? We must change these kids' lives and give them opportunity!
>
> — JOSHUA THERRIEN

TIP #187: The term sexting comes from combining the words "sex" and "texting." By the simple click of a button on a phone or online device, a sexual message is sent from one person to another. With this same simple action, a nude image of someone can also be sent to another person. As foster parents, we cannot be afraid to discuss hard subjects like this with our foster children.

> Ask yourself this at least once a week: How can YOU be a better advocate for our children in need?
>
> — JOHN DEGARMO

JULY 7

TIP #188: In many parts of the world, the possession of sexual images of a minor is a criminal offence—a serious one at that, as it is deemed child pornography. Along with this, knowingly or intentionally possessing visual material, such as naked pictures, that depict a minor engaging in sexual conduct is also a crime. It is important that you share this information with your foster youth, as she may not appreciate or fully understand the legal danger of sexting and similar activities.

> After all, the gift of love is one that can be shared, not only during the holidays, but all year long.
>
> — JOHN DEGARMO

TIP #189: Let your foster child know that you will
not accept any inappropriate sex talk, whether in your
home or through online technology and social media.
Inform your child that you will closely monitor his
online actions as well as his cell phone for any disturbing
messages, texts, and pictures. As you check your foster
child's online devices on a regular basis, be on the
lookout for sex-based messages. Remember, you are not
invading the child's privacy; instead, you are helping
keep the child and the child's privacy safe.

> Don't hold onto your thoughts in silence, speak out,
> share, and find the supports around you.
>
> — CONNIE GOING

TIP #190: Any time a child talks about suicide, it should be taken very seriously and you must report it to the caseworker immediately. Document what was said, when it was said, the emotional state of the child, and how you responded. There are times when children in foster care threaten suicide as a way of gaining attention. However, even if you suspect this you must report it to the caseworker immediately.

> People say, 'He's so lucky to have you.' The truth is I'm so lucky to have him.
>
> — ANONYMOUS

TIP #191: Take your foster child to new places to have new adventures. It is likely that the child placed in your home has not had opportunities to go out to dinner, to the movies, to amusement parks, or similar places. Take your foster child out to do these things; introduce her to new things and new adventures. This not only helps her to feel like part of the family but also introduces her to new experiences and opportunities that she may only have while living with you.

> You can discover more about a person in an hour of play than in a year of conversation.
>
> — PLATO

JULY 11

TIP #192: Play ball! Encourage your foster child to join a sports team of some kind. Whether it is a school-related sports team or a community-based one, sports can be a great opportunity for a child in foster care. Not only are sports fun and healthy, they also allow foster children to make new friends, develop social skills, and heal through play therapy.

> Being a parent is tough. Being a foster parent is even tougher.
>
> — JOHN DEGARMO

TIP #193: One important rule your child from foster care can learn while playing sports is that of good sportsmanship. There is a good likelihood that no one has ever taught your foster child this before. Teach the value of playing fair and that winning is not always the objective. Praise him for his efforts on the field or court, his hard work, and for his commitment—not for his wins and losses.

Be kind to unkind people—they need it the most.

—ANONYMOUS

TIP #194: You aren't always in control—live with it. Many foster parents struggle with the fact that they can't control everything. From visitations to court appearances and from child behavior to eating habits, you are not in charge of many things that will happen regarding your foster children. Much of it is simply beyond your control, like when your foster child will leave.

> It is worth all the effort you are putting into being a parent.
>
> — JOHN DEGARMO

TIP #195: Don't allow the bureaucracy and the system to get you down. As a foster parent, you will quickly learn that fostering comes with a great deal of paperwork. On top of that, there is often a level of bureaucracy that coincides with caring for children in foster care. You may find that the "system doesn't always work," and this can be both challenging and depressing. Yet, focus on how you can best help your child each day, and try not to let the state policies and the system frustrate you.

> It is a happy talent to know how to play.
>
> —RALPH WALDO EMERSON

TIP #196: Learning never stops. There are many good books available about foster parenting and foster care. Some are lighthearted, while others take a more academic approach. Perhaps you need one to help you learn more about your child's developmental issues. Maybe you need to learn more about the dangers that children in foster care face with social media. Perhaps it is time you read an inspirational book. Whatever it is, find a good book that will help you with your foster parenting questions and struggles right now.

> Life isn't about finding yourself. Life is about creating yourself.
>
> — ANONYMOUS

TIP #197: What you do is not easy and can be very stressful and time consuming. Go ahead and treat yourself today to something nice. Buy a carton of your favorite ice cream flavor—all for yourself. Indulge in your favorite chocolate or candy. Buy yourself a cup of coffee at your favorite coffee shop. Take yourself out to lunch. Order a season of a new TV show to watch on your laptop or tablet. You deserve it!

I am thankful that you have opened up your home and your family to children who need help, who need stability, and who need love.

—JOHN DEGARMO

TIP #198: Create a Lifebook for the child placed in your home. Lifebooks contain your child's life story, and they can be an important link to her life and family before coming to live with you. Think of it as a scrapbook for children in foster care that helps to hold their life together as they move from home to home.

> A day without sunshine is like night.
>
> —JOHN DEGARMO

TIP #199: A Lifebook can help you, as the foster parent, better get to know the child placed in your home. As you work with them to create this Lifebook, the relationship between the two of you can be strengthened. When you help your child create their Lifebook, you help him keep in touch with his past and birth family.

> Each day of our lives we make deposits in the memory banks of our children.
>
> — CHARLES R. SWINDOLL

TIP #200: As a Lifebook is a scrapbook of sorts, you will need an actual scrapbook, glue, scissors, crayons, and colored pencils. Additionally, try to find pictures of your foster child—both from before she came to live with you (if possible) and from while she is with you. Any certificates she has can also be included, like any certificates or documents from school, sports, etc.

> Do not read as children do, to amuse yourself, or like the ambitious, for the purpose of instruction. No, read in order to live.
>
> — GUSTAVE FLAUBERT

TIP #201: If you are having a difficult time getting pictures of your foster child from when he was younger and before he came to live in your home, ask the child's caseworker or any former foster parent that he lived with. When possible, also ask the child's birth parents or biological family members for pictures. As the two of you collaborate together to help the child, you strengthen your relationship with the birth family and develop a trust.

Each foster child who comes through your home will remember one thing: that for a period in his life, he was loved. And some day down the road he will blossom into something better because of it.

— JOHN DEGARMO

TIP #202: Include pictures of your child's birth parents in their Lifebook, if possible. Make no mistake: this is important, as these people remain her parents and family. If your child no longer has contact or a relationship with her birth parents, these pictures will grow even more important as your child grows older. Also include pictures of siblings, other biological family members, former foster parents or caregivers, special caseworkers, and anyone else significant in her life. Try and identify each person by writing their name under their picture.

> The soul is healed by being with children.
>
> — FYODOR DOSTOYEVSKY

TIP #203: Take steps to make sure that the wording in your foster child's Lifebook is age appropriate. Also, make sure that the pages are not cluttered or filled with too much information. Instead, keep it neat and simple.

As you read this, there are children who are falling prey to child sex trafficking.

— JOHN DEGARMO

TIP #204: Family history is important to each of us, and it is to your child from foster care as well. At some point in his life, he will want to know about his family and where they came from—this is very normal. Include any and all family history you might know about your child in their Lifebook. Ask the caseworker or birth parents about your child's family tree. Additionally, find out if any of your child's family members held interesting careers or jobs or served in the military or in a war, and include this information in the Lifebook.

> Where there is love there is life.
>
> — MAHATMA GANDHI

TIP #205: Your foster child's medical history is very important. If she should move from home to home and family to family, this type of history and information is essential. Yet it is easy to lose this type of information during transitions. Get information from the caseworker and biological family members about your foster child's medical history, along with her family members' histories. You may have to piece this information together, but the effort is necessary.

Children make you want to start life over.

— MUHAMMAD ALI

TIP #206: Part of the fun of a Lifebook is showcasing your foster child's accomplishments and successes. Include positive report cards, quizzes and tests, homework, and other school related paperwork that showcase his successes. If he should receive any certificates of accomplishments for sports, music, art, or other activity, include these in the Lifebook, so he can look back upon these in later years.

> When you share God's love with a child in need, you are changing the life of a child, and changing the world.
>
> — ANONYMOUS

—————

TIP #207: Pictures of happy events are a must for every Lifebook. Include any pictures of birthday celebrations and holidays—make sure these are in the book. If your child has dressed up in silly costumes for Halloween, parties, or simply around your house, include those pictures. Pictures of any pets that your child has formed an attachment with while living in your home should also be included. Don't forget pictures from when your child went to an amusement park, camping, shopping, or to other fun events in her life.

> The flower that blooms in adversity is the rarest and most beautiful of all.
>
> — ANONYMOUS

TIP #208: A letter from an important person in your foster child's life would be a great addition to their Lifebook. This letter can be about how important the child is in that person's life. Perhaps a letter from a caseworker, former foster parent, teacher, church leader, birth parent, or other special person could be included. Your child can re-read that letter over and over again and it can be a source of comfort for him.

> A characteristic of the normal child is he doesn't act that way very often.
>
> —ANONYMOUS

TIP #209: As this is your foster child's Lifebook, work with her to include information about what the child likes. Her hobbies, interests, favorite foods, favorite toys, things she misses from earlier in her life, and her hopes and dreams for the future.

> I wanted to help those children who were at risk, as did my wife, and thus our foster parenting experience began.
>
> —ANONYMOUS

TIP #210: Remember, this is not your Lifebook. This Lifebook belongs to the child from foster care that is placed in your home and you should allow him to make it himself—with your help. It can be a little messy to create, so it may not be the most perfect or cleanest book. It might not be the book you planned or envisioned at all, and that's okay.

> Building the inside up first gives way for that needed experience and confidence necessary to transition into normalized activities.
>
> — T.J. PETRI

TIP #211: Supervision never stops. From time to time check in on your child, wherever she might be. Whether she is in her room, outside, in the basement, or anywhere else, continue to look in on her. Not only will you be able to better monitor her and her activities, you can also provide comfort to her, as it shows that you care and are concerned for her well-being.

> Never doubt that a small group of thoughtful, committed citizens can change the world; indeed, it's the only thing that ever has.
>
> — MARGARET MEAD

TIP #212: It is only normal that if you have a foster teen living with your family, he will want to have his own sense of identity and even some independence from you and your family. It is okay for you to allow your foster child to be a teenager. Give him permission to try and fit in with the other students at school with clothing styles, as long as they are appropriate. You might really disagree with your child's sense of style and clothing, but remember, your own parents might have disagreed with yours when you were that age as well.

> It wasn't until I had my first child from foster care living with my family that I came to fully understand the tremendous challenges that these children face.
>
> — JOHN DEGARMO

TIP #213: A lack of gratitude is not uncommon for teens in foster care. The teen in your home may not appreciate all that you do for her and will seldom thank you for meeting her needs, providing for her, and showing her kindness and love. Do not take this personally, as she very well may struggle with trying to trust anyone, let alone you.

Children seldom misquote. In fact, they usually repeat word for word what you shouldn't have said.

— ANONYMOUS

TIP #214: Can he trust you? This is one question that your foster teen is most likely asking about you. Whether you are his first placement in a foster home or he has had several placements, your foster teen may feel like he has been betrayed by all the adults in his life. He may build up walls and attempt to protect himself from further pain and betrayal. As a result, you will most likely have a hard time breaking through these walls and gaining your child's trust. In truth, he may feel that he has no reason to trust you. Trust takes time and your foster child needs that from you.

> Broken trust is like a melted chocolate; no matter how you tried to freeze it, it will never return to its original shape.
>
> — ANONYMOUS

TIP #215: Be prepared for a difficult time with a foster teen. Your foster teen may try to break many of your rules and make your life as miserable as possible in the hope of you asking that she be removed from your home. Often, foster teens believe that if this happens, they will be returned to their biological family members. During this hard time, your foster teen will need you to be patient with her, support her, and understand that she is suffering and in pain.

> Very little is needed to make a happy life; it is all within yourself, in your way of thinking.
>
> — MARCUS AURELIUS

TIP #216: Doubt but do not give up. Foster parenting is hard, and there will be times that you doubt what you are doing, doubt that you are making a difference, and doubt that you are a good parent to a child in need. These are thoughts that many parents experience. Don't give in and don't give up. Instead, recognize that there will be challenges and that you are not perfect. The child in your home does not need you to be perfect, he just needs you to care about him and protect him from harm.

> Let's begin to break this cycle of failure and sadness for our children, and instead create an atmosphere of success and understanding.
>
> — JOHN DEGARMO

TIP #217: Sit down with your family and discuss safety issues such as medicine being locked away in cabinets, seat belt use while in moving vehicles, electrical outlets, and other concerns. It is important not only for your foster child but for your entire family to routinely inspect your home for any problems that could bring harm or danger to those living in your home. Check fire alarms, electrical outlets, locks, windows, and other features on a consistent basis. Keep a fire extinguisher in your home for emergencies and make sure that your foster child knows what to do in the case of a fire.

> Happiness consists in activity. It is a running stream, not a stagnant pool.
>
> — ANONYMOUS

TIP #218: Remember, you are not a perfect parent. You will make mistakes from time to time, and you will look back and wish you had done some things differently. This is normal. You are not perfect; there is no perfect parent. But, you are trying your best. More importantly, you are providing a child the love that she needs. Simply learn from your mistakes and don't second guess yourself. You are doing a great job.

> Enjoy life. This is not a dress rehearsal.
>
> — ANONYMOUS

TIP #219: For so many children, school is a place of learning, of laughter, and to make friends and form relationships. Not so for children in foster care. It can be a very difficult place where academic failure and behavior problems are the norm. It can be a place of humiliation, bullying, shame, and sorrow for those who are placed in a foster home. Even the best schools are the last place they want to be. For the foster child who has been taken from his family, from his home, from his friends, and from all he knows and suddenly placed into a strange home late one evening only to be forced to attend a strange school the following day, school is incredibly traumatic. It is important that you keep this in mind when a new child is placed into your home.

A child is a curly, dimpled lunatic.

— RALPH WALDO EMERSON

TIP #220: Expect the foster child in your home to struggle in school—both academically and in behavior. Many children placed under foster care supervision suffer from at least one learning-based developmental delay. Many other children in the custody of child welfare agencies exhibit the need for special education services. In addition to this, students in foster care exhibit an array of academic difficulties, including cognitive abilities that are weaker than traditional students. Federal and state funding to assist in this problem is lacking, as well.

> After a few foster children had passed through my own home, I began to appreciate the fact that I had to not only adjust my teaching habits for foster children, but I also had to become my own foster children's advocate at their own schools.
>
> —JOHN DEGARMO

TIP #221: Be aware that your foster child may suffer from falling behind in school. Most children in foster care are on average about eighteen months behind in school and academics. Thus children in foster care not only suffer from learning disabilities, but fall behind each time they move from one home to another. When a child is absent from school, she falls behind in the classroom. When children in foster care miss more and more days of school due to multiple placements, they fall further and further behind. High levels of absenteeism frequently lead to grade retention, which leads to frustration and behavioral problems. Those children who experience multiple placements in a short time may face the dilemma of not obtaining special help regarding specific services to assist them with learning disabilities/impairments, as schools often do not have the time necessary to implement appropriate testing.

> There is nothing in a caterpillar that tells you it's going to be a butterfly.
>
> — R. BUCKMINSTER FULLER

TIP #222: Enrolling your child from foster care into a new school can be difficult. When your child moves from one home to another and from one school to another, it becomes difficult to place him in the proper classes that he needs. Many times, school records and transcripts do not accompany the child when he is placed into a new home. When you go to enroll your foster child into his new school, you may be missing these important records and transcripts. As a result, schools may not know what classes to place your child in or the educational services he might require. If your child does not have his transcripts and school records with him when he is placed into your home, ask the caseworker for them.

What is a home without children? Quiet.

— HENNY YOUNGMAN

TIP #223: Your expectations of your foster child's school behavior and academic success must be reasonable. Many children in foster care may not care about their school work, their grades, or how they behave in school. This will not magically change overnight once a child is placed into a foster home. In fact, it may take a very large length of time for a student in foster care to change her attitude toward school after she is placed into your home. Indeed, she may not change her attitude toward school at all while under the supervision of foster care—or even for the rest of her life. This may be because the child has lived in an environment or home for many years where school was not stressed as important.

It is never too late to be what you might have been.

— ANONYMOUS

TIP #224: The relationship between a foster child's caseworker and their teachers is often not as strong as it should be. Caseworkers often have difficulty obtaining information regarding the foster child's performance in the classroom, as schools are often reluctant to release this information to caseworkers or are unable to do so because of state legal issues. When caseworkers cannot obtain the needed information, they have to rely on you, the foster parent, for information regarding the status of the child's progress at school.

> As foster parents, we have the opportunity to help bring families together, to help children heal, and to help biological family members be better parents and caretakers.
>
> — JOHN DEGARMO

TIP #225: Teachers are often not made aware of the emotional challenges that foster children face. Foster children come with a myriad of emotional issues and many teachers are simply not equipped to handle them. Foster children may lash out in the middle of class and many teachers do not have the training or the resources to handle these challenges. Foster children often have trust issues with adults as well as issues building healthy relationships with adult figures. Thus, the relationship between teachers and foster children is quite often unhealthy. Your child's teachers need you to support them.

> Whoever is happy will make others happy, too.
>
> — ANNE FRANK

TIP #226: When you enroll your child into his or her new school, request to meet with his new teachers, school counselors, and administrators. During this time, deliver as much personal information about the child as you are allowed and permitted to. This includes important information about your child's foster history, behavioral challenges, and learning disabilities he might struggle with. If you know of any behavior modifications that work for your foster child, go ahead and share these, as well. The more information you are able to share with the teachers, the more understanding, compassionate, and flexible they are likely to be when working with your child during troublesome moments. In addition, this helps to build healthy relationships between the teachers and your child from foster care, thus helping them succeed in school.

> Children are natural mimics who are like their parents despite every effort to teach them good manners.
>
> — ANONYMOUS

TIP #227: Your foster child needs you to be the best advocate for her at all times—including when she is in school. You can help your child from foster care by reaching out and forming a positive working relationship with your child's teachers and maintaining contact with them on a consistent basis. Go ahead and let your child's school counselors, teachers, and administrators know that they can call you when necessary and when needed. This will be the most helpful for teachers— reassure them that you willing to work alongside them in regards to your child. If you feel comfortable, give your phone numbers, email address, and contact information to the school. At the same time, ask for the phone numbers, email addresses, and contact information of the child's teachers and counselors.

Happiness is not a goal; it is a byproduct.

— ELEANOR ROOSEVELT

TIP #228: Being a child in foster care is hard. When you notice that your child is having a particularly difficult time or is struggling at home, reach out to the teachers and school counselors to simply let them know. Perhaps you can let these teachers and school counselors know a little about why he is struggling or about the difficulties he is facing and how you have addressed it. This information will help prepare the teachers and counselors in advance—before your child comes into their classrooms and into school—and better prepare them to handle any difficulties that might come their way. A little advance warning, if you will, can go a long way in helping teachers better understand why your child might be acting in a challenging way or misbehaving. This prior knowledge also helps teachers to better understand your child in general, as well.

> As a foster parent, you can teach life lessons and help both child and parent learn new skills. What a great opportunity and, at the same time, a big responsibility.
>
> — JOHN DEGARMO

TIP #229: There are times when visitations between your child from foster care and her birth parents and biological family members may be difficult and emotionally distressing to her. These difficult visitations can cause additional emotional anxieties and concerns for her, both before and after a visitation. As your child struggles to manage the many emotions that are swirling inside of her about these visitations, her anxieties may spill over into the classroom. As you can imagine, focusing on school work will be difficult for her. Along with that, she may struggle with her behavior as she tries to manage her emotions.

Where are the loud voices protesting that the government give rights to children? When will we fight to protect the children in our own nation?

—JOHN DEGARMO

TIP #230: When you are proactive, you can help both your foster child and his teachers. During those times that your child is struggling with the emotions revolving around visitations with birth family members, you can help by informing his teachers before a visitation takes place—giving them some advance notice. A quick note in a school agenda, an email, a text message, or a phone call are all ways that you can let your foster child's teachers know in advance that your child may be struggling with difficult emotions and thus struggle in the classroom.

Girl, n. A giggle with glitter on it.

—ANONYMOUS

TIP #231: See if you can reschedule that event. As you know, children in foster care miss too many days of school—for a number of reasons. When it appears that your child might miss even more school due to a scheduled visitation, a court appointment, or even a medical appointment, ask your child's caseworker if the appointments can be moved to after school or on weekends, in order not to miss any more days of school. Stress to the caseworker that you are concerned that the child might fall even further behind. Though this recommendation may not be met by the caseworker, it is important for you to try. You never know; your request might be approved.

> Children are likely to live up to what you believe of them.
>
> — LADY BIRD JOHNSON

TIP #232: Your encouragement matters. Many children in foster care have never had anyone encourage them to set goals or even to look towards the future. As a foster parent, you should always encourage your child to set some goals—both in school and in life. You may be the only adult who has ever given him any confidence and words of encouragement about school and his classwork. At the same time, it is important that you do not push him beyond his abilities. If you do, it will only frustrate both of you all the more. Sit down with him and ask him to share with you what success means for him, then find ways to help him find that success. At every opportunity, celebrate every single success he accomplishes in school, no matter how big or small. Each success is reason to celebrate.

> Every child deserves to be loved.
>
> — JOHN DEGARMO

TIP #233: Get rid of your foster child's distractions and give her a special place. She may struggle with focusing on her schoolwork and studies, as she is instead focused on wanting to go back home. Remind yourself that there are many emotional distractions for her and that these interfere with schoolwork. Help your child by setting up a special homework station. Find a place that is away from distractions—such as television, video games, and other media—that may interrupt her concentration. Think about setting up her very own office some place in your home with a desk, school supplies, and a bulletin board with lists of upcoming projects and school due dates.

> The best way to cheer yourself up is to try to cheer somebody else up.
>
> — MARK TWAIN

TIP #234: You are a model. One way to show your child from foster care that schoolwork is important is to model it. When your child has homework or studying to do, this might be a great time for you to work on your own projects (if you are taking classes of your own), or for you to take time to sit down and read a book. Allow him to see that reading is a normal part of your life and that it is both fun and important.

> Parents can only give good advice or put them on the right paths, but the final forming of a person's character lies in their own hands.
>
> — ANNE FRANK

TIP #235: Schoolwork is most likely going to be diffi-cult for your child, and she will need your help. Each day, take time to go over her work and assignments with her. Make sure that she truly understands what needs to be done and that she understands the directions. Ask your foster child if she has any questions and try to answer those as best as you can. Most children in foster care struggle with reading and math. As a result, she might need you to read the directions or help with her work. You might also need to help her study and prepare for quizzes and tests, as no one may have taught her these skills before.

I am inspired by your service to others, and placing those in need before yourself.

— JOHN DEGARMO

TIP #236: Reading never gets old and a child can never get enough reading. There may be some days that your child's teachers do not assign him any schoolwork. When this happens, encourage him to read a book of his choice. You can ask him to read it either out loud to you or quietly to himself. Like all children everywhere, children in foster care need to read, as it helps to develop so many skills and interests, and opens up new worlds of learning, thinking, and imagination to them. Once again, your foster child may have never had anyone read a book to him. Therefore, try to do just that each day. Help him develop and strengthen his reading skills. In fact, he will need you to help him develop this skill, as it will be one that he will use the rest of his life.

> A mother understands what a child does not say.
>
> — PROVERB

TIP #237: Socializing in school and in public may be a skill that your foster child never truly developed. Yet, it is one that is essential for her well-being, safety, and success—not only while she is in school and living with you, but for her future, as well. She will need to rely upon these socializing skills in her classroom each day, as she interacts with her teachers and fellow students. Along with this, she will need to rely on these same skills when she is older and applies for a job, looks for a place to live, and in all aspects of her life. The development of these social skills will also help her to withstand times of difficulty and challenge in her life—again, both in school and in the future.

> When you come to the end of your rope, tie a knot and hang on.
>
> —ANONYMOUS

TIP #238: One way of helping your foster child to develop positive social skills is to model them each day. Remember, he is watching what you do and listening to what you say each moment. So instead of just telling him how to act in certain ways, show him how to do so by what you say and do—both in your home and while you are out in public. Model these skills in all that you do, each moment, so that he can watch and learn from you.

> Children are great imitators. So give them something great to imitate.
>
> —ANONYMOUS

TIP #239: "Please" and "thank you" still matter. Teach the child in your home to use good manners at all times. Remind her that saying "please" and "thank you" to others never goes out of style. In fact, it is not only good manners but is an important social skill as well. It is likely that these words are foreign to her, as she may have lived in a home where negative and harsh comments were the norm. Instead, teach her that old familiar saying: "If you have nothing nice to say, don't say anything at all."

> Any kid will run any errand for you if you ask at bedtime.
>
> — RED SKELTON

TIP #240: Many children who have come from homes of abuse and neglect have a difficult time maintaining eye contact and looking at someone when spoken to. This not only includes with you, but with his caseworker, therapist, teachers, and fellow students. Teach him why it is important to look someone in the eye, give him opportunities to practice with you in your home, and compliment him when he is successful. Along with this, help him to focus on paying attention to conversations, how to focus on what is being said, and not to interrupt others who are talking.

> The most important thing a father can do for his children is to love their mother, and the most important thing a mother can do for her children is to love their father.
>
> — ANONYMOUS

TIP #241: Personal space and privacy go hand in hand. These may be skills that you need to reinforce on a regular basis to your foster child. She needs to learn from you that each of us has personal boundaries and personal space and how not to invade those spaces and boundaries. At the same time, make sure you do not invade her personal space and boundaries—be sensitive to these.

> The key to a family is to be open to the possibilities, to embrace the realities, and above all, enjoy the children you have been blessed to parent.
>
> — RACHEL GARLINGHOUSE

TIP #242: Music soothes those that are both restless and savage. Indeed, music can be a great way for your foster child to learn, heal, and grow for a number of reasons. Music helps to develop communication skills and also helps to improve self-confidence. Music can help a child to develop independence. Concentration and attention skills are also developed and increased through listening to music, and finally, music helps children learn to become more self-aware of not only themselves, but also of others.

> Children are a great comfort to us in our old age, and they help us reach it faster too.
>
> — ANONYMOUS

TIP #243: Continue to introduce the children in your home to various styles of music. Have some sort of music playing in your home throughout the day. Find fun music to sing to and sing along with it. Make music a fun and regular part of daily life in your home.

> Take time to grieve, and remind yourself that you are not in control of the situation.
>
> — JOHN DEGARMO

When I was forty-nine years old, I ventured into the complexities of the foster-adoption process, praying that God would bring the child he wanted me to have into my life. My daughter then entered my life at seven years old, unapologetically desiring a family. She was (and still is) funny, caring, and loving with a strong-willed spirit. Our connection was strong and remains so today—eight years later. However, our journey together has had its ups and downs. At one point, I realized that my daughter needed greater support than I could provide. I had become tired, frustrated, and empty and had to make one of the hardest decisions I've had to make: I placed her in a full-time residential environment where she could receive intensive support and develop better coping skills. She was angry and I felt guilty, as she had already experienced loss and I did not want her to feel abandoned. Like most parents at one point, I doubted my parenting skills. However, during the time apart I learned how to take care of myself emotionally, physically, and spiritually. She learned how to cope with her emotions and behaviors and developed more independence. Once we were together again, we both learned to communicate better and I learned to establish clear expectations and boundaries and hold her accountable for her actions. Our family is now stronger than ever.

— TRACI

TIP #244: Students who have taken music classes and studied music and the arts generally have higher grades and perform better on tests. One way to make music a part of your foster child's life is to introduce a musical instrument to him. Give him a harmonica, sign him up for piano lessons, encourage him to take music class in school, and even talk to him about joining the high school marching band. Music teaches so many lessons— in so many different ways.

> For me, the partnership with my spouse is essential in so many ways, and I would not be a good foster parent if not for her.
>
> — JOHN DEGARMO

TIP #245: Sometimes, failure is a great learning opportunity. As a foster parent, don't rush to try and fix everything that goes wrong for the foster child in your home. Allow her the opportunity to fail and to try to learn from it. Give her a chance to discover her own way of fixing the problem and finding a solution. This will allow her to develop problem solving skills as well as self-reliance.

> Happiness comes when your work and words are of benefit to yourself and others.
>
> — BUDDHA

TIP #246: Admit it when you mess up. Your child needs to learn how to apologize, and one of the ways he can best learn is from watching you. When you make a mistake, when you break something, when you hurt someone's feelings, or even when you lose your self-control, apologize to your child and admit that you were wrong. Remember, you are the role model, and this is a great opportunity to be an example to a child who has probably never heard a parental figure say they were sorry.

> Real life is about being there to listen, to comfort, to sit in their pain with them. Not pretending that we know what they are feeling or telling them what they can do different.
>
> — SATY CORNELIUS

TIP #247: Love your spouse, especially in front of the kids! It is very likely that your own marriage is the only example that your foster child has of what a healthy marriage and relationship should be and look like. When he is older and considers getting married, he will have your relationship and marriage as an example. Don't be afraid to hug, kiss, and compliment your spouse in front of your child. You are setting the example for his future relationships.

> A strong foster parent is one who is not afraid to say "I love you" to his or her own spouse, to his children, and to her foster children.
>
> — JOHN DEGARMO

TIP #248: Social skills need to be taught every day. One of the ways you can teach social skills is to help your foster child develop strong communication skills. Ask her questions each day that he can answer. After school, ask him what the best part of school was and what the worst part of school was. At dinner, ask him questions about what he is looking forward to tomorrow. At bed time, ask him to read a book to you. Look for ways to build his communication skills throughout the day.

> Attitudes are much more important than aptitudes.
>
> — ANONYMOUS

TIP #249: Comparisons can hurt. Do not compare one child with another, whether the two are living together in your home or in separate homes. Don't say things like, "Why can't you have good grades like Steven?" or "Maria is so much better behaved than you. Try to act more like her." These types of comments only suggest to your foster child that she is not good enough or that she is second rate.

> Home is a state of mind. Home is a knowing, beyond the shadow of a doubt, that someone loves you and will always be on your side — even when trust comes hard and self-worth seems fleeting.
>
> — MICHELLE MADRID-BRANCH

TIP #250: Your enthusiasm is contagious, and your foster child needs to be infected with it. You might be the first adult to show encouragement to your foster child. Make sure you tell him throughout the day how much you appreciate him—and do it with enthusiasm. Tell him what a great job he did cleaning his room, doing his homework, brushing his teeth, and helping around the house. Look for opportunities to show your enthusiasm and excitement about him.

Practice random beauty and senseless acts of love.

—ANONYMOUS

TIP #251: Remember that your mealtime and family diet will probably not be familiar to your foster child. Do not be surprised if she is not interested in eating what you prepare, or if she fights about what is for dinner. You are in charge of the meal and your family diet. Continue to prepare healthy, nutritious meals for your family—even if she doesn't want to eat it. Even if she refuses to eat, don't give up. Our bodies know instinctively when to eat and she eventually will. She won't starve if you continue to provide opportunities for her to eat a balanced diet.

> There is a child who needs me. There is a child who will make me a better person at the same time, as well.
>
> —JOHN DEGARMO

TIP #252: Make mealtime family time. As busy as your lifestyle is and as much as you have to do each day for yourself and your family, try to find time to eat at least one meal everyday together, as a family. When you sit down at the dinner table together as a family, it is a great way to connect with each other. Make it a time to share enjoyable stories, exciting news, engaging conversation, and even a funny joke or two. This not only helps your child to develop heathy eating habits, but it also helps to create social skills and build relationships and trust.

> What if you helped one child today? What if the world looked better because of what you did today?
>
> — JOHN DEGARMO

TIP #253: Allow your foster child to plan the menu. Once a week, give him the opportunity to choose the meal. Whether it is his favorite meal of macaroni and cheese, frozen pizza, or even pancakes at dinner time, give him the opportunity to not only choose what's for dinner, but to help you cook and prepare it as well. By allowing him this weekly choice, your dinner time battles during the rest of the week may be alleviated.

Children are our most valuable resource.

— HERBERT HOOVER

TIP #254: Co-parenting is part of the job. Many foster parents find it difficult to work with their foster children's birth parents. When a foster parent shares the nurturing of a foster child with the birth parents and caseworker, reunification tends to happen at a quicker and more successful rate. Co-parenting sees you, as a foster parent, working alongside the biological parents of your foster child and with your family.

Try and look for joy in each moment.

— JOHN DEGARMO

TIP #255: It is important to always keep in mind the cycle of abuse. For many children in foster care, their parents suffer from personal traumas and anxieties from their past. Many biological parents of foster children were abused themselves and know of no other way when raising children. Additionally disturbing is that some birth parents were foster children themselves and are just repeating the cycle they went through as a child.

> It is easier to build strong children than to repair broken men.
>
> — FREDERICK DOUGLASS

TIP #256: Never pass judgement on your foster child's birth parents. When you do, your foster child will certainly suffer.

Though no one can go back and make a brand-new start, anyone can start from now and make a brand new ending.

— ANONYMOUS

TIP #257: You may find that there are some biological parents who will be happy to work with you in order to be reunited with their child. Additionally, these birth parents may want to learn better parenting skills. You might also discover that they are grateful that you are taking care of their child during this time and that their child has enough food, is safe, and is cared for.

A wish changes nothing. A decision changes everything.

— ANONYMOUS

TIP #258: While some birth parents may be grateful that you are caring for their child, others may not be so appreciative. Indeed, they may be angry with the child welfare agency and feel that their child was taken away unnecessarily. Along with this, some birth parents may feel resentment toward you, as their child is living in your home and not theirs. In their eyes you might be "the bad guy" and the enemy, thus they may look to find fault with all you do.

> You might be the only one who brings love and joy to a child. Embrace that heavy responsibility.
>
> — JOHN DEGARMO

TIP #259: As you know, you are a role model to your foster child in so many ways. You are also a role model to the birth parents and biological family members. To your foster child's relatives, you might be the best example of what a good parent is. Everything you do as a foster parent will send signals to the biological parents on how a parent should act as well as how to treat their children. They are learning from you by what you say and what you do toward their child—and in all that you do.

> Happiness is when what you think, what you say, and what you do are in harmony.
>
> — MAHATMA GANDHI

TIP #260: The end goal of foster care is for reunification between the child and her family. While it does not always happen, chances are that this is the wish of both your foster child and her family. As a foster parent, you should support reunification of your foster child and her biological parents. You can show this support by finding ways to help the biological parents with their parenting skills. Discuss ways and ideas about how you can help them meet their caseload, as they attempt to meet the requirements of reunification.

Real courage is displayed by those who are afraid to go, but go.

— ANONYMOUS

TIP #261: There will be questions for you from your foster child's birth parents, as they are curious about you. Your foster child's birth parents will want to know what kind of family their child is living with, what his home life will be like, if he is being taken care of, and many other concerns. After all, their child has been taken away from them—against their wishes—and placed in a strange home. They will have many concerns and may not be as courteous to you as you might like. Be prepared for them to be hostile, rude, angry, or even distant. Remember, they are hurting and have been through a traumatic experience with the removal of their child.

> One thing I have learned over the years as a foster parent is that I must be flexible.
>
> —JOHN DEGARMO

TIP #262: One way to work with your child's birth parents is to look to them for advice. After all, they are the experts on their child. Have a list of questions ready for them when you first meet them; questions that will show to them that you are not only interested in their child, but that you want the very best for him. By indicating with your questions that they, as his parents, are the experts, you will begin to form an important relationship—one that will benefit all involved.

> A man can fail many times, but he isn't a failure until he gives up.
>
> —ANONYMOUS

TIP #263: You might include the following questions when you meet with your foster child's biological family members:

- Is she on any medication?
- Does she have allergies to anything in particular?
- Has she had chicken pox?
- What are her favorite subjects in school?
- What subjects does she struggle with?
- Does she have any behavior problems?
- Does she have any fears?
- Can she swim?
- What are her favorite foods?
- What are her interests?
- If she is young, does she have a favorite toy?
- Does she have any particular religious practices?
- Does she have a regular routine at home?

Kids don't remember what you try to teach them. They remember what you are.

— JIM HENSON

TIP #264: Your foster child's parents will want to know that their child is happy, healthy, safe, and cared for in your home. You can help them feel at peace by reassuring them that their child is safe in your home, as well as given plenty of positive attention and love by you. In addition to this, tell them that you are excited to have their child in your home while they are working on their case plan. They may also want to know more about your own family. Let them know about some of the traditions in your home. The more reassurance your foster child's birth parents have that their child is in a good home, the better your relationship with them will be.

> When you are born into a world where you don't fit in, it's because you were born to help create a new one.
>
> — ANONYMOUS

TIP #265: Visitations are an important part of the re-unification process for your foster child and his biological family members. Visitations are scheduled face-to-face meetings between the child and his biological parents or family members. These visitation meetings can be held at a number of neutral locations; a community park, a church, or a child welfare agency are all possible locations. During the visitations, your child's caseworker, or other social worker, has the opportunity to assess the foster child's relationship with his parents or family members, give the parents a chance to practice parenting skills, and gain insight into how the parents are progressing in regards to reunification.

> I don't worry because I understand the other side of coming out of a cocoon is a beautiful and fulfilling life.
>
> — CONNIE GOING

TIP #266: Visitations are one way your foster child can heal. As she attends visitations with her biological family members, your foster child will likely feel that she has not been abandoned by them. As a result, her own self-worth and importance will be bolstered, too. As she continues to visit with her birth family, you may also find that her behavioral problems and anxiety levels decrease in your home and in school.

> Is it pandemonium in our house? Perhaps. Is it a house that is never fully clean? Without a doubt. Is it a house full of love? Absolutely!
>
> — JOHN DEGARMO

TIP #267: Looking one's best is always important. Your foster child should always look his best when he has a visitation with his birth parents. Help him get dressed in nice, clean, and appropriate clothing. Make sure his hair is washed and combed and that his appearance is top notch. If he has a cold, don't be afraid to give him a little cold or cough medicine before the visitation, as nobody wants him sneezing or coughing on anyone else. Finally, make sure you arrive on time—or, better yet, early—to the visitation. All of this will help send the message to the birth parents that you not only care for their child, but that you consider visitations with them important.

> The more risks you allow your children to make, the better they learn to look after themselves.
>
> — ROALD DAHL

TIP #268: Be prepared for your foster child's visitation to cause some anxiety and even sadness. Your child's heart can certainly be broken during visitation if the birth parents should not show for some unexplained reason. Another source of emotional angst for your foster child may be if her birth parents should speak negatively about you. This may lead to your child struggling with feelings of loyalty for both you and her birth parents. Finally, your foster child may be let down by unfilled promises or false hopes given by her birth parents.

> Life is like riding a bicycle. You don't fall off unless you stop pedaling.
>
> — CLAUDE PEPPER

TIP #269: Safety first! Part of protecting your foster child is making sure your house is safe. Make sure there is a fire extinguisher within easy reach on every floor of your home. Routinely inspect and test the batteries on your fire alarm detectors. Never leave a child under the age of six in the bathroom and bathtub alone. Check to see that all medicine cabinets are sealed and locked. Ensure that all child seats in your car are installed correctly.

Make time to smile today. The child in your home needs to see it from you.

— JOHN DEGARMO

TIP #270: TV or not TV. There is no reason why your foster child should have a TV in his room. Research has shown that children who have televisions in their bedrooms sleep less, perform poorer in school, have more difficulty with social skills, and even weigh more. Keep the TV in a central location in your home where you can monitor what is being watched.

What if the children in your home never saw you laugh? What might that be teaching them about life?

— JOHN DEGARMO

TIP #271: There is a time and place for everything, even as a parent. One place that a child should not be punished or reprimanded is in public. If your child is making poor choices or is misbehaving, try to redirect her behavior. If the behavior continues, find a private place or spot to speak to her. If you punish her while in public, this will only serve to embarrass her and perhaps only escalate the behavior. Feel free to praise your child for any accomplishments or good behavior while in public, though. A kind word in public goes a long way.

> There is more to ourselves than we even realize.
>
> — SATY CORNELLIUS

TIP #272: When your foster child feels he is ready to talk, ready to open up to you, or ready to share his concerns and emotions with you, you need to be ready to listen. He may be ready at a time that is not necessarily convenient for you and your schedule. Nonetheless, stop what you are doing and give him your undivided attention.

> Love who you are — and who you are not.
>
> — ANONYMOUS

TIP #273: It's okay to have a messy house. Give your-self permission to have a house that is not always clean. Allow your child to make a fort out of blankets, pillows, and other items. Children like to make forts and it allows them to use their powers of creativity and problem solving skills. Indeed, it is even okay for your child to sleep in her fort overnight, as long as you decide that it is safe and that she will come to no harm. You can always have her clean up in the morning. And remember—chances are you made a fort when you were a child, as well.

> Whether it is a newborn baby or a teenager, our foster children are just like other children: active and seemingly into everything!
>
> — JOHN DEGARMO

TIP #274: As your foster child may have come from a home where he suffered from neglect, he needs words of comfort and love from you at all times. One of the ways you can do this is to greet him each morning with a smile and a "good morning." Perhaps even sing a good morning song when you wake him up in the morning. When he goes to bed, another smile and a "good night" from you can help to make him feel loved and cared for.

> We do not remember days; we remember moments.
>
> — CESARE PAVESE

TIP #275: Ever feel like you are losing your mind while foster parenting? No, you are not. Even when things are the most difficult and challenging, even when your stress level is at its highest, even when the noise level is at a roar, this hard time will pass at some point. Try to find ways to relax, even in the most challenging of times; breathe and remind yourself that this too shall pass.

> To raise a child who is comfortable enough to leave you means you've done your job. They are not ours to keep, but to teach how to soar on their own.
>
> —ANONYMOUS

TIP #276: Who gets to choose? One way to solve the problem of who gets the bigger piece of cake (or larger scoop of ice cream, etc.) is to employ the "I cut, you choose" formula. One child cuts the slices of cake or pie (or scoops the ice cream into bowls), while the other gets to choose which one is hers. This simple act encourages the first child to cut or scoop into fair and equal portions. It is a simple yet effective way of teaching a child how to be fair.

> Children learn more from what you are than what you teach.
>
> — W.E.B. DUBOIS

TIP #277: Table manners never go out of style. Not only is it likely that your foster child is not used to eating at the dinner table as a family, it is also likely that he is not familiar with table manners. Teach him how to hold a fork, knife, and spoon properly. Show him how to fold a napkin in his lap. Remind him to cover his mouth when he has to cough or belch. If he needs to leave the dinner table during a meal, teach him to ask to be excused. Finally, when mealtime is over, ask him to help clear the table, push in his chair, and help clean the dishes.

What is a child learning from you today?

— JOHN DEGARMO

TIP #278: So many children in foster care have difficulty falling asleep or having a good night's sleep. This should really be no surprise, as the anxieties that children in foster care face can often overwhelm them. For some children, their brains are always on alert and they are never able to escape the worries and concerns they have. This is due to the abuse, trauma, and neglect that they may have suffered before coming to live with you. As a result, they feel that they have to be alert to protect themselves from additional harm and abuse.

Do not educate your child to be rich. Educate him to be happy, so that when he grows up he knows the value of things not the price.

— ANONYMOUS

TIP #279: Sleep time can be a scary time. For those children who have experienced traumatic events in their lives, bedtime can be a time when they relive those memories and experiences once more. Your foster child might have a fear of being alone or of the dark. Perhaps she is afraid of unfamiliar and scary noises. She may also feel that she is being abandoned when left alone in her bedroom. In addition, sleep can bring recurring dreams—which may force her to relive a traumatic event time and time again.

> Making the decision to be a foster parent is a difficult one. It takes incredible commitment, unconditional love, and patience.
>
> — JOHN DEGARMO

TIP #280: Bedtime can be an exhausting time for you, as the foster parent. When your foster child struggles or resists going to sleep each night, it can affect your own sleeping habits as well as your entire family's. Sleep is important to your well-being and is essential to your health. When your foster child won't sleep, it is likely that you won't either. Finding ways to help bring a good night's sleep to your foster child is not only important to him but to your entire family.

> Human happiness and moral duty are inseparably connected.
>
> — GEORGE WASHINGTON

TIP #281: Routine is important in so many areas of your foster child's life, including sleep time. One way you can help your foster child to find a good night's sleep is to have a consistent bedtime routine each evening. Find activities that are calming and soothing before bedtime; make them activities that he engages in on a consistent and regular basis. Skip the TV, video games, and online technology, as these often include bright lights, flashing images, and loud noises.

> Your love as a foster parent is quite essential to the child's health, well-being, and future.
>
> — JOHN DEGARMO

TIP #282: Part of your nightly routine can include bath time, brushing teeth, and even story time. Story time with your foster child each evening before bedtime not only helps to establish some quiet time, it also helps her to refocus on positive stories and images, allowing her to leave behind some of the traumatic memories she might be struggling with. In addition, when you read out loud to your foster child, it helps to improve her vocabulary and brain development. Lastly, reading a book to her can also help her to develop her own love of books and of learning.

> For I was hungry and you gave me something to eat, I was thirsty and you gave me something to drink, I was a stranger and you invited me in. I needed clothes and you clothed me, I was sick and you looked after me.
>
> — MATTHEW 25:35–36

TIP #283: Avoid stimulants around bedtime. Not only should your foster child avoid TV, video games, and computers, he should also avoid other stimulants such as caffeine, energy drinks, and candies before going to bed each night. In addition, some over-the-counter cold and cough medicines as well as other prescribed medications may also contain side effects that pertain to sleepless nights. If you believe that some medicines that your foster child is taking might cause him to have sleepless nights, ask your doctor or physician about these and ask for other suggestions.

> We have to be there for them, especially when they push us away.
>
> — ASHLEY RHODES-COURTER

TIP #284: Make no mistake, the first few nights in your home can be very confusing to your foster child. Not only should you have a nightlight in the bathroom so that she can locate it in the dark, but you should have a nightlight in her bedroom. However, ensure that the nightlights are not so bright that they keep her awake at night.

> 'I must do something' will always solve more problems than 'Something must be done.'
>
> — ANONYMOUS

TIP #285: Calming music at bedtime can help to soothe a child into slumber. When a child is anxious, worried, or troubled, music can be a great influence in restoring peace to your foster child's mind. Consider having calm and soothing music playing quietly in the background of his bedroom. Perhaps you can even hum or sing softly to the child as you sit on the bed next to him as he falls asleep.

I have come to realize that the gift of children is a precious one, and that the responsibility of raising children is one that is so very important.

—JOHN DEGARMO

TIP #286: Set limits. Bedtime does not necessarily mean question and answer time. Your foster child may have some questions for you when she goes to bed or want to talk about some concerns on her mind. Try to limit this conversation time and not engage her in too much talk during bedtime. Tell her that you would love to spend some one-on-one time with her tomorrow or another time, but now is bedtime. However, you need to be flexible with this rule, as bedtime might be the time that she finally opens up to you or expresses some legitimate fears that need comforting.

> Among all the noise and the activity, I take time to simply bask in the moment of time with the children, celebrating their presence in my life.
>
> — JOHN DEGARMO

TIP #287: A gentle reminder can go a long way toward a good night's sleep. At bedtime, your foster child may feel that he is all alone and has been deserted once again. Remind him before you say your final good night that you are still there, still around. Keep the door open if he is little and look in on him from time to time. Reassure him with your presence that he is not alone.

> Time is the best teacher.
>
> — ANONYMOUS

TIP #288: Pick your bedtime battles. Just like other areas of discipline, you should pick your battles when it comes to bedtime. If your foster child wants to read in bed for a little while before falling asleep, it is okay to allow this. After all, he is staying in bed quietly, is learning, and is developing an appreciation of books.

> There have been moments when I have questioned whether or not I was making a difference. We all have those moments. It's okay.
>
> — JOHN DEGARMO

TIP #289: Look for natural remedies to help your foster child sleep. The use of the natural hormone melatonin has been a popular remedy for those who struggle with sleep. This natural hormone is made by the body's pineal gland, and it helps the body recognize when it is time to sleep and when it is time to wake up. If you decide to use melatonin to treat your foster child, check with your doctor first to see if it is okay.

> It is not attention that the child is seeking, but love.
>
> — SIGMUND FREUD

TIP #290: Another natural sleep aid is lavender. Studies have shown that lavender helps the body to relax and that the scent of this natural herb can help the sleeping process. If your foster child is struggling to sleep, lavender might be one way to treat this challenge.

> A day of worry is more exhausting than a day of work.
>
> — JOHN LUBBOCK

TIP #291: Weighted blankets are also known to help children fall asleep and may be helpful for your sleepless foster child. These specially designed blankets often have a weighted material sewn into them, sometimes between two layers. These noninvasive blankets are designed to help those who suffer from insomnia or anxiety. The pressure from these weighted blankets affects the brain, as the pressure helps to release neurotransmitters. This in turn helps to improve the person's mood and brings about a calming effect.

> What if each of us took time to make a difference for a child in need? My, how the world would look different.
>
> — JOHN DEGARMO

TIP #292: While the act of play can be enjoyable for a child, it can also be very therapeutic and healing for a child who has suffered from abuse. Yet, it is important that you monitor your foster child's pretend or imaginary play. Check to see if she is acting out acts of sexual abuse or using oversexualized themes. Look to see if she is pretending to be bullied or hurt by imaginary friends. Check for signs of other forms of inappropriate themes in her play. If you find these, document them and make sure you alert your caseworker; your foster child may need to see a trained counselor.

> It's critical to understand that love does not conquer all.
>
> — RACHEL GARLINGHOUSE

TIP #293: So many children today find their entertainment through video games. One way you can help your foster child learn to better socialize and communicate with others is by teaching them to play an old-fashioned card game or a board game of some sort. Show your foster child how to put down the computer and play a game of cards instead.

Anything scarce is valuable; praise for example.

— ANONYMOUS

TIP #294: The statistics are not positive for youth who age out of foster care. In some states, youth in foster care age out, or leave the system, at eighteen years of age. In other states, it may be twenty-one years of age. On average, fifty-five percent of youth who age out of foster care will never receive a high school diploma, sixty-five percent will end up homeless, and seventy-five percent will face some time incarcerated. As a foster parent, it is important that you prepare your foster child for the time that he reaches adulthood.

> Even if people are still very young, they shouldn't be prevented from saying what they think.
>
> — ANNE FRANK

TIP #295: Perhaps like you did, most young adults leaving home for the first time have someone that they can rely on and turn to when facing challenges. Whether these problems are financial, emotional, school oriented, or work related, most young adults can pick up a phone and call an adult who is quick to help. Foster children who age out of the system do not often have this type of support. Part of being a foster parent is being this person and this type of support for one of your foster children later on.

> To be in your children's memories tomorrow, you have to be in their lives today.
>
> —ANONYMOUS

TIP #296: You can greatly help your foster child by teaching him important living skills. Skills such as cooking meals, driving a car, finding housing, keeping appointments, managing a bank account, shopping for groceries and household items, and even taking public transportation are missing in many children who age out. Allow your foster child to learn how to cook for himself. Teach him how to clean and take care of a household.

> Surely, there is no earthly reason to be a foster parent. So, why do we do it? For many, like my wife, we are answering a call. The call to take care of children who are hurting, who are scared, who are in need.
>
> — JOHN DEGARMO

TIP #297: As soon as your foster child is ready, start teaching her the basics of personal financial responsibility. Show her how to develop simple money skills. One exciting way to do this for her is to help her open up her very own personal bank account. She will need you to teach her not only how to manage her own account, but also how to manage money in general.

> History will judge us by the difference we make in the everyday lives of children.
>
> — NELSON MANDELA

TIP #298: Help stop the generational cycle present for so many foster children. Talk to your foster teen about the realities of being a parent—and do so on a consistent basis. Encourage him to choose options and activities that will focus his attentions and point him toward a positive future, such as school clubs, sports, music, and theater. Be consistent in their lives on a daily basis and make yourself available for conversation on this topic—and any other topic they might wish to discuss.

It is a wise father that knows his own child.

— WILLIAM SHAKESPEARE

TIP #299: Go ahead and gossip. Your foster child needs your praise and encouragement, but you can also help her self-esteem by allowing her to overhear you gossiping about her in public. Share some of the accomplishments of your foster child with your friends, your church members, the caseworker, her teachers, and others. When she overhears you bragging about her, it will help her feel better about herself and give her confidence.

> Life is a shipwreck but we must not forget to sing in the lifeboats.
>
> — VOLTAIRE

TIP #300: Never allow your foster child to speak to you, members of the family, or any other person in a tone of disrespect. Though he may be hurting inside, never permit him to speak rude or hurtful words to you or others. If he should choose to do so, let him know that this type of speech is not accepted and that he can do much better. Keep in mind that this type of talk might be normal for him, due to his environment before being placed in your home.

> All little girls should be told they are pretty.
>
> — MARILYN MONROE

TIP #301: Every year, thousands of children in foster care are adopted by their foster parents. Perhaps you are considering adoption or have already adopted a child from foster care. Adoption Day parties are a wonderful way to celebrate your foster child officially joining your family. Invite friends and family members over on the day that the adoption is final, and celebrate the event with cake, ice cream, balloons, and presents—making it similar to a birthday party. Show her how important she is and that the adoption is a special day for not only her, but for your whole family.

> My family has not only grown in size through adoptions, they have grown in love, as well.
>
> —JOHN DEGARMO

TIP #302: It is important to recognize that the simple act of adoption, however joyous it can be, can also bring about forms of depression. Your foster child may struggle with the knowledge that he will never return to live with his biological parents or birth family members again. It will be very necessary for you to allow him time to not only process and accept this, but also to grieve the loss of connection with his birth family.

> Just because a foster child finds a forever family when he is adopted does not mean that it will be smooth sailing afterwards, or that there will not be difficulties or challenges ahead.
>
> **— JOHN DEGARMO**

TIP #303: One way that you can help your adopted child process her feelings of grief and loss is to allow her to discuss these feelings with you. If your child should ask any questions about her biological parents or birth family, answer them as honestly as you can. In addition, it is important that you help her to transfer attachment from her birth family to yours. Include her in every aspect of your family, as she is now part of your permanent family.

> Don't go through life, grow through life.
>
> — ERIC BUTTERWORTH

TIP #304: If possible, and if all involved feel comfortable, consider having an open adoption. An open adoption allows open contact between the biological parents and the foster child, allowing a one-on-one relationship to be possible as they interact directly with each other. Communication may consist of letters, emails, social networking sites, phone calls, and even visits. Open adoption benefits both sides, especially the child, as it permits him to resolve any feelings of loss and relationship and gives him access to information that he might seek later on in life.

> It took me four years to paint like Raphael, but a lifetime to paint like a child.
>
> — PICASSO

During the last five years, I have been serving young adults who have aged out of the foster care system. Quite often these "kids" come with funky attitudes and can be very challenging to get along with. For example, we recently welcomed two young men into our home to live with us. During the first month of their stay, one of these young men spent a weekend in jail for previous arrests, tried to steal our car, and was swarmed by security at the social service office. (Apparently he had been previously banned from the office when he'd threatened the workers.) However, one night we had some "family" time as we all got together to talk with a young lady who needed a home. After she left, this troubled young man looked at me and said, "Ms. Maurita, I want your home to always be home for me." What more can I ask for? Foster parenting is the hardest thing I have ever done but is definitely the most rewarding. When I hear words like that, it causes me to sit and think about the children that have come through my door and the impact they have had on me—and I on them.

— MAURITA

TIP #305: Remember that age matters and that some children act older than their actual age. Your foster child may have had to act as a parental figure in her home either for herself or for others, for one reason or another. Keep in mind the actual age of your foster child and treat her accordingly. Allow her the opportunity to enjoy life at the age she is. If she is young, allow her the chance to play and be a child. If she is older, allow her the benefits and opportunities that go along with her age, if appropriate.

> Whether you are a foster parent, a social worker, or one who simply cares for all children and wants to be a stronger advocate for them, may you share your gifts with others.
>
> — JOHN DEGARMO

TIP #306: Laughter is good medicine. The life of a foster parent can be difficult, can be emotionally draining, and can be stressful at times. Yet, there are moments of joy, of success, and of surprise. For your own health and well-being, and for that of everyone living in your home, work to make sure that you don't take everything so seriously. Learn to laugh—not only at the funny moments but sometimes at the absurd and unexpected. There are times when it is okay to laugh at the light side of things. Along with this, find moments to laugh alongside your foster child; help him to develop a healthy sense of humor, as well.

> A child miseducated is a child lost.
>
> —JOHN F. KENNEDY

TIP #307: Patience is a virtue you need to have. Teenagers are bound to be emotional and moody. It's normal for them, and it is normal for all parents to have challenges during this phase of their child's life. Your foster teen will probably be moody and emotional, as well as overly sensitive. Along with that, she may question everything you do and say and remind you that you are not her real parent. Indeed it is a difficult age for foster children, as they struggle to have a normal life like their peers. Be patient and remind yourself not to take anything personally.

> There are two primary choices in life: to accept conditions as they exist, or accept the responsibility for changing them.
>
> — DENIS WAITLEY

TIP #308: Take time to appreciate the ride and the journey. Yes, it can be hard, and yes, you might not see the difference you have made in your foster child's life. At the same time, foster parenting is an enjoyable experience. You are able to watch a child heal and grow, you get to meet others who share the same desire to help children in need, and seldom do you experience a moment of boredom. Take time to enjoy the experience, and reflect on all that has happened in your life and the life of the child in your home since he became a part of your family.

> There will be moments when you are exhausted, worn out, and frustrated. At the same time, there will be those moments when you are filled with laughter, joy, and love. Foster parenting will bring you all of these emotions, and so much more.
>
> — JOHN DEGARMO

TIP #309: Don't forget to take care of your vehicle! As a foster parent, you are bound to spend a lot of time driving from one place to another. Whether it is a trip to the doctor's or to the therapist, a visitation or a court hearing, going to the child welfare office or to a foster parent training session, you will place many miles on your car. Have your car's oil changed, tires rotated, and engine checked on a regular basis.

> An obstacle is often a stepping stone.
>
> — WILLIAM PRESCOTT

TIP #310: Many churches and faith-based organizations help children in foster care as part of their outreach programs. Some ways these faith-based organizations and churches have helped foster parents and their foster children include: collecting new or donated clothing, toys, bedding materials, and other necessities for foster children; donating school supplies and backpacks for foster children; helping to support local foster parents with meals, transportation, etc.; and even helping to pay for summer camps and field trips for foster children. Ask your caseworker if there are faith-based groups in your area that help, and seek them out. They are there to help you and the foster child in your home.

> For one full week, these foster children had me as a counselor and as a mother, and we made memories and we became stronger. What I was doing was the most important thing in the world; I was investing in their well-being.
>
> — SUSAN MCCONNELL

TIP #311: Respite care can be a great help to you as a foster parent. There may be times when you need a short-term break from your foster child. Perhaps you had a vacation planned for some time before the child was placed in your home and you can't cancel it. Maybe you need to travel out of the state in an emergency. Maybe your own children need to have a weekend with just you for some much-needed special time. Perhaps you are trying to prevent burnout and need a break from your foster child for a short time.

> Indeed, foster parents DO need rest and a time of reprieve, every now and then.
>
> — JOHN DEGARMO

———————

TIP #312: Respite can be a confusing time for your foster child if she is not prepared beforehand. You can help make this short-term transition much easier and much less stressful for her by doing a few things. When you find that you need respite care, first contact your caseworker and ask for help finding a placement for your foster child.

> It is okay for you to take time for yourself, your spouse, and your family. It is okay to recharge those batteries.
>
> —JOHN DEGARMO

TIP #313: If you have the opportunity, visit the respite family with your foster child beforehand. This will allow you to ease any concerns and fears your foster child might have—especially if your foster child has attachment issues. Talk with the respite family and ask when the best time to drop off your foster child is, and inform them when you would like to pick your child up after the break is over. Finally, while he is in respite care, contact him daily if you can. You can do this through phone calls or text messages—simply to remind him that he has not been deserted.

If you cannot do great things, do small things in a great way.

— NAPOLEON HILL

TIP #314: Perhaps one of the most difficult moments of being a foster parent is the moment when your foster child leaves your home. As a foster parent, you have been able to provide a home where your foster child has come to find a place to heal, find a place to discover hope, and find a place to be loved. Yet, at some point, the child will most likely leave your home. Each year, over fifty percent of foster children are reunited with their parents in what is known as reunification. Around ten percent of children in foster care will go to live with grandparents, aunts and uncles, or other members of their biological family. Eighteen percent of foster children will end up being adopted, while fewer than ten percent will age out of the foster care system upon turning the age of eighteen.

All men know their children mean more than life.

— EURIPIDES

TIP #315: There might come a time when you personally request for your foster child to be removed from your home. Make no mistake, this is a very difficult decision. Possibly your own children and foster children are simply not getting along like you had hoped. Perhaps you feel as if your foster child is harmful to your family or is a dangerous influence on your children. You may find that you are unable to properly care for her.

> If not us, who? If not now, when?
>
> — ANONYMOUS

TIP #316: When your foster child leaves your home, it can bring about feelings of loss and grief—and it hurts. Rest assured, these feelings are normal for foster parents. Do not ignore or dismiss them. When any foster child leaves your home, no matter the level of attachment, there will be emotions when it is time to say goodbye—for both you and the child.

> As we watch our favorite reality TV shows, there are children who are being abused so horrifically that many of us turn away; the reality of it too gruesome for us to acknowledge.
>
> —JOHN DEGARMO

TIP #317: Your heart may break when you have to say goodbye to your foster child. Foster parents do feel grief during the removal of their foster child, and this should come as no surprise to you. After all, your foster child has come to be an important member of your family and one you may have come to love deeply. When he leaves your home, it is a loss, and any loss can cause grieving.

> Saying goodbye is never easy for anyone and may be especially difficult for you and your foster child.
>
> — JOHN DEGARMO

TIP #318: Whenever a loved one leaves home, emotions of grief and sadness are normal. There are other times, though, when you might be angry with the removal. Perhaps you don't believe that removing your foster child from your home only to place her into another one is the right thing to do. Perhaps this leaves you concerned for your foster child's safety. You might believe that the home the child is moving to is unsafe, unstable, and even unhealthy for her. Remind yourself that these decisions are often out of your hands, as they are made in a court system and by a judge.

> Enjoy the little things, for one day you may look back and realize they were the big things.
>
> — ANONYMOUS

TIP #319: Grief can be expressed in a variety of ways and depends upon the individual, as it is personal. Some will shed tears and cry, while others hold it inside. Some will busy themselves in a task, while others will seem detached and far away. The departure of your foster child from your home can be an event that is devastating to you and your family.

> Children are the living messages we send to a time we will not see.
>
> — JOHN F. KENNEDY

TIP #320: In order to help treat your grief, it is important that you know the stages of grief from Kubler-Ross: denial, anger, bargaining, depression, and acceptance. This will allow you to understand the feelings that may come with the removal of your foster child from your family. At the same time, realize that these very feelings may have been felt by your foster child when he was removed from his home and first placed in yours.

> It can only take a moment to waste the rest of your life.
>
> — CHUCK PALAHNIUK

TIP #321: The feelings of shock after a foster child's removal from your home can be overwhelming. After a foster child has formed an emotional attachment to the family, her sudden removal may cause deep shock and uncertainty, leaving your family confused.

> It's okay to take some time off to grieve the loss of a foster child from your home and from your life.
>
> — JOHN DEGARMO

TIP #322: If you feel denial after a foster child is removed from your home, this does not mean that you do not feel any grief. When a child suddenly moves from your home—for whatever reason—you might deny that you ever truly formed a relationship with your foster child. You might also deny that you feel any sadness. Though you may deny your feelings, you might be grieving deeply with the belief that you were unable to provide the help the foster child needed.

> If you make children happy now, you make them happy twenty years hence by the memory of it.
>
> — ANONYMOUS

TIP #323: You may experience feelings of anger when your foster child is removed from your home and family. This anger and severe disappointment might be directed toward your child's caseworker as well as the child welfare system. You might even place blame upon the system in general, the caseworker for the placement, or someone that you believe is harmful to the child.

> When we love children in foster care with all that we have, we help them to begin to heal.
>
> — JOHN DEGARMO

TIP #324: Be aware that guilt is another stage of grief. You may blame yourself and believe that you are at fault for your foster child's removal. It is during this time that you may struggle to understand what you might have done "wrong," and believe that it was your fault in some way. Furthermore, if you had to request that your foster child be removed for the protection and well-being of the rest of your family, you may feel guilty. You may believe that you were unable to care for your foster child and that you failed him in some way.

> It takes a village. And I just want to wake that village up because we are powerful in numbers. The world's orphans need us not to slumber while they suffer.
>
> — MICHELLE MADRID-BRANCH

TIP #325: After a child leaves your home, you might try to substitute the grief you feel with the actions of trying to help others in need. This might be done in an attempt to justify the loss of your foster child. Additionally, you might request another placement of a new foster child— and in quick fashion—hoping to substitute one child with another and leave behind those feelings of grief. Yet, in truth, you cannot replace one child with another. Be aware that your grief will surface at some point.

> That's what people do who love you. They put their arms around you and love you when you're not so lovable.
>
> — DEB CALETTI

TIP #326: Depression is a normal stage of grief. When a child is removed from your home, it is natural that you experience some form of depression. However, there are different components to depression brought on by grief. You might become easily irritated; experience a constant state of feeling tired or fatigued; feel as if you can no longer continue with your day-to-day life; or even have a difficult time with normal tasks with your family, your marriage, your friends, and at work.

> Changing diapers, feeding babies, doing dishes, and even reading bedtime stories are all gifts in disguise.
>
> — JOHN DEGARMO

TIP #327: It takes time to properly heal, and time does heal many wounds. After time has passed, your grief from the loss of your foster child will decrease. With this passage of time you will be better able to accept and understand the reasons behind the removal of your foster child. Additionally, your emotional well-being will improve. Again, give it time.

> Be happy while you're living, for you're a long time dead.
>
> — SCOTTISH PROVERB

TIP #328: One thing that can help when you are experiencing feelings of grief and loss as a foster parent is to surround yourself with those who understand you best. The only people who will truly understand you and appreciate what you go through as a foster parent are other foster parents. When you join a foster parent association or support group, the group gives you the opportunity to find the support system you need and deserve. Along with that, a foster parent support group helps you to develop relationships and friendships with other foster parents just like you. These relationships and new friendships are great opportunities for you to validate your own experiences and emotions while caring for children from foster care in your home.

> It is wise to direct your anger towards problems — not people; to focus your energies on answers — not excuses.
>
> — WILLIAM ARTHUR WARD

TIP #329: Foster parent support groups are a no judgement zone. Most of your friends and family will not completely understand what you do as a foster parent, and some might even pass judgement upon you and your choices. When you join a foster parent support group or association, you will be able to share with fellow foster parents the challenges, frustrations, and difficulties that you feel and experience—all without judgment. In addition, you can laugh along with them at some of the craziness that comes with being a foster parent, vent your frustrations to those who understand, and cry in front of a group of people who truly appreciate what you are going through. You will find the support and encouragement that you need when you face the unique challenges and difficulties that go along with being a foster parent.

> Perhaps there is a child near you, right now, who is waiting, and even praying, that you fight for their human rights.
>
> — JOHN DEGARMO

TIP #330: Your foster parent support group or association can provide you with the chance to learn from others who have lived your same lifestyle: your fellow foster parents. As you listen to their stories and experiences during the group meetings you will be able to learn from them, and gain wisdom from how they may have handled a situation that you struggle with. Another bonus from joining a foster parent support group is that you can share ideas and resources with each other. Don't be afraid to join a local foster parent support group. It may be just the support you need.

> Whether you're a foster parent to one or two or eight, at whatever age, the first priority should be building foundations.
>
> — ANAIS NIN

TIP #331: Don't be afraid to use writing as a way to treat your grief. Journaling is a popular way that many foster parents address their own feelings of grief and loss. When you write about your thoughts, feelings, and emotions and put those thoughts into words on paper, you allow yourself to release your emotions in a manner that is private and personal. By doing this, you are able to express yourself and process your feelings. When grief is not processed in some way but is instead bottled up inside, feelings and emotions become suppressed—which leads to more emotional problems in the future.

Dreams are necessary to life.

— ANONYMOUS

TIP #332: Know your "personal calendar dates." Specific calendar dates may trigger overwhelming feelings of grief and loss for you. When the birthday of your former foster child comes up on the calendar, this reminder can be a painful memory of the child that is no longer living with you. Furthermore, certain events and milestones of the child, along with holidays, can cause feelings and memories of the child to be revived within you. You need to be aware of your own personal calendar dates, or those dates that correspond with a foster child of yours in some way, and prepare your expectations for the feelings and emotions that might be triggered within you.

> All who would win joy, must share it; happiness was born a twin.
>
> — LORD BYRON

TIP #333: Preparation is important. The moment your foster child leaves your home can be a time of great difficulty and one of emotional upheaval. As a foster parent, it is essential for all involved that you prepare. From the very first day you bring a foster child into your home, it is crucial you remember that she will most likely not live with you forever. At some point, she will move from your home and family to another home, perhaps through reunification with her birth parents or biological family members, or with another family altogether. With this in mind, it is very important that you plan for her departure before that time arrives.

> Love opens the door to a heart that is in pain.
>
> — JOHN DEGARMO

TIP #334: Remember that Lifebook you created for your foster child? Before he moves, make sure that it is up-to-date with the latest pictures, memories, school reports, and other information that will be important for him in his new life and new home. Include pictures of your own family in it, making sure that each person pictured is named. Along with this, include your contact information, as he may want or need to reach out to you in the future.

> The whole world is my family.
>
> — POPE JOHN XXIII

TIP #335: Your foster child will naturally be curious and even anxious about the family she will soon be moving to. Questions about her future family are normal. You can help her by finding out as much information about her new home and situation as you can. If you are able, get the phone number of the family she is moving to, perhaps from the caseworker, and call the family beforehand. Introduce yourself to them and allow your foster child to speak with them, so she can familiarize herself a little with them before the move. If she is moving back to her biological family, this phone call will help in easing this transition, as well.

> You have abilities, gifts, and experiences that equip you for foster parenting.
>
> — JENN AND TJ MENN

TIP #336: Time for a party! Consider giving your foster child a going away party in order to show him how much he will be missed by you and others. Invite his caseworker, friends, teachers, church members, friends of the family, and anybody else over that played an important part in his life during the time he lived with you. You might also give him some going away presents that he can remember you by. These presents can be both enjoyable—like toys, books, games, etc.—and practical—like clothing, shoes, school supplies, toiletries, etc. Make his going away party a fun and memorable one, and show him how important and cared for he is.

> They say love hides in every corner, then I must be walking in circles.
>
> —ANONYMOUS

TIP #337: Help your foster child pack when she prepares to move from your home. If possible, try to get her a new suitcase. So many children arrive into a foster home with all of their possessions in a black plastic bag. When she leaves your home, give her the gift of a new suitcase. Help her fold her clothing and belongings into the suitcases. If she has a lot of toys or large items, you may have to use boxes as well. Make sure you pack everything she owns, including everything she came into your home with. Add some stationary, pencils, and pens so that she has everything she needs to write to you.

A little extra attention from you to a child goes a long way.

— JOHN DEGARMO

DECEMBER 4

TIP #338: After your foster child moves, you will most likely miss him. He will probably miss you, as well. You can help ease his anxieties during this time by reaching out to him. Allow him to tell you about his new home and family. If you have children of your own, encourage them to talk to him. Writer him a letter and send him pictures of your family from time to time. Of course he will want to be remembered on his birthday, so send him a birthday card and gifts and call him on the phone.

> Children are the bridge to heaven.
>
> — PERSIAN PROVERB

TIP #339: Make sure you have an emergency escape plan in place in case of a fire or other emergency. Practice using this emergency escape plan with all the children in your home, so they can be prepared for such an emergency. Your emergency escape plan should have two exits from your house. Make sure that your foster child knows where to go if an emergency occurs and where to meet up once outside. Your foster child has probably come from a home that did not have an escape plan. Assure her that you have this plan so that she will be safe in an emergency—and that she is safe at the moment.

> Let us reach out to the children. Let us do whatever we can to support their fight to rise above their pain and suffering.
>
> — NELSON MANDELA

TIP #340: Swimming is a lesson that can last a life time. If your foster child does not know how to swim, give him the gift of swimming lessons. Not only will he find pleasure and enjoyment in swimming once he learns how , it can also be a source of good exercise for him, help build his social skills, and build self-confidence. Of course, knowing how to swim could also one day save his life.

> I wasn't planning on loving you. I am so glad I was wrong.
>
> — JOHN DEGARMO

TIP #341: Holiday time might not be a time of joy for your foster child. Christmas, Hanukkah, New Years, Kwanzaa, and other holidays can be very difficult times for foster children. While the holidays might be a time of great joy and holiday cheer for you, your foster child might instead be faced with the realization and the reminder that she is not with her own family and will not be "home for the holidays," so to speak (with her own biological family). Indeed, when she is surrounded by people who may be strangers—strangers who are having fun—the holiday may be a difficult day for her.

> When they leave our homes, we should grieve for them, as it simply means that we have given them what they need the most: our love.
>
> — JOHN DEGARMO

TIP #342: As a foster parent, you will need to help prepare your foster child for the holiday times beforehand. Prepare him before Thanksgiving, before Christmas, before Hanukkah, and before family members and friends come to visit. It is necessary for her well-being and understanding, as well as for your own family, that you address what to expect with your foster child.

> The love of a family is life's greatest blessing.
>
> — ANONYMOUS

TIP #343: No doubt your foster child will feel some anxiety about living in your home during the holiday time. You can begin to help him by allowing him to talk about what he might be feeling during the holiday season. Make sure you check in on him often and ask him how he is doing. Understand that he may not be happy and might not be enjoying this special time like others in your family are.

> When you feel unloved, look at me and you'll know without a doubt that you are loved.
>
> — WHITNEY GILLIARD

TIP #344: Christmas, New Year's Eve, and other holidays can be a depressing time for children in foster care. Look for signs in your own foster child of depression, sadness, and similar emotions during these times. After all, she may be grieving the fact that she is away from her biological family members and living with strangers.

> Therefore do not worry about tomorrow, for tomorrow will worry about its own things. Sufficient for the day is its own trouble.
>
> — MATTHEW 6:34

TIP #345: During the holiday time, your foster child may need time alone. Allow him space to privately grieve if he needs to. Don't insist that he take part in every family tradition that you have. Additionally, be prepared if he should revert back to some behavior difficulties he had when he was first placed in your home. Along with this, he may become upset, rebellious, or complain a great deal. After all, he is trying to cope with not being with his own family during the time when families most often get together. Feelings and actions like this are normal for a child who is filled with tremendous anxiety.

A baby will make love stronger, days shorter, nights longer, bankroll smaller, home happier, clothes shabbier, the past forgotten, and the future worth living for.

— ANONYMOUS

TIP #346: We all seem to have a crazy uncle, obnoxious cousin, or embarrassing relative. Your family is used to these relatives and has learned how to put up with their unique personalities. However, it is important to remember that your foster child is not familiar with that unique relative with perhaps an overwhelming personality. During the holiday time, your foster child may feel even more stress from this type of relative.

> Children in foster care need people on their side, from the time the sun comes up to the time they go to bed.
>
> — JOHN DEGARMO

TIP #347: If family members and relatives visit your house during the holiday season, you will want to prepare your foster child for this. Remind her that the normal routine she has become adjusted to in your home might change and even become a little "crazy" during your family's visit. As it might get loud and chaotic in your home during this time, be patient with your foster child if she should withdraw, lash out, or struggle in general. Remember, your relatives are strangers to her, and she is missing her own family while you are surrounded by your own.

> Trust because you are willing to accept the risk, not because it's safe or certain.
>
> — ANONYMOUS

TIP #348: Although your foster child may struggle with his emotions and behavior during the holiday season when you have family and relatives visit your home, it is important that you continue to model good behavior and good manners for him. Remind him that even though the house might seem overly crowded and noisy, he is still expected to use good behavior and manners. If he should act out or speak rudely toward others, remain patient and loving toward him.

> One can pay back the loan of gold, but one dies forever in debt to those who are kind.
>
> — MALAYAN PROVERB

TIP #349: Most likely those visiting your home during the holidays will not be familiar with the realities of foster care, and they may have misconceptions about children in foster care. Additionally, they may not understand or appreciate the day-to-day challenges that your foster child faces. More so, they might not see her as a member of your family and may treat her differently. Take time to explain to your family and relatives that she is a member of your family and that she should be treated as such.

> The meaning of life is to find your gift. The purpose of life is to give it away.
>
> — ANONYMOUS

TIP #350: As your holiday visitors may not fully appreciate or understand foster care and foster parenting, they will likely have questions for you about the foster child placed in your home and living with your family. Gently remind them not to ask your foster child questions about why she is there or what happened to her. In fact, ask your visitors not to fire questions at her at all. Instead, if they have questions, encourage them to ask you. Only share with them what you feel comfortable telling—and what you're legally able to tell.

> The act of adopting a child allows us to be God's hands and feet for those children who have no family to call their own.
>
> — JOHN DEGARMO

TIP #351: The subject of gift giving during the holiday time can be a tricky one for both foster parent and foster child. Your holiday visitors, if you have them, may not understand that your foster child is part of your family and that you treat him like your own child. Be prepared that some of your family and relatives may not have gifts for him but bring gifts for the other members of your family. Quite likely, your relatives either did not remember he was living with you, did not know, or just did not appreciate that he is a part of your family at this time.

> It's nice to be important, but it's more important to be nice.
>
> — ANONYMOUS

TIP #352: Be ready for the fact that your family and visitors may not have gifts for your foster child when they visit your home during the holiday season. They may have no presents for her at all, or may not have the same amount as they do for your own children. Whatever the reason, have some extra gifts already wrapped and hidden away somewhere, ready to be brought out just in case. If you do need to bring them out, don't draw attention to it, as it will be embarrassing for all involved. Instead, simply say that the gifts are from the relatives.

> Want to leave a legacy of love? Learn to serve others.
>
> — JOHN DEGARMO

TIP #353: Your holiday visitors will have questions about your foster child, and that's normal. Their questions are probably well intended and not meant to be rude or intrusive. Look at questions from your holiday visitors as ways for them to better understand your foster child's background or how the foster care system works. Also, be prepared for such questions.

> Blessed are those who can give without remembering and take without forgetting.
>
> —ELIZABETH BIBESCO

TIP #354: As you answer the many questions about your foster child and about foster parenting from your friends and family members, remember what is confidential. There are some things about your foster child that need to remain private. Never say anything that might embarrass your foster child, and do not reveal information that is intended to remain confidential. Instead, take these questions as an opportunity for you to bring better awareness about foster care and how others can help children in need.

> The truth is, a fire in my heart has been lit to help children in foster care.
>
> — SUSAN MCCONNELL

TIP #355: Your foster child may wish strongly to see his birth family and biological parents during the holidays. Despite all the abuse and trauma that he might have experienced from them, his desire to see them during this time is quite normal. Talk to your child's caseworker about arranging opportunities for your foster child to visit his birth family during the holiday season. Make time for this and don't let your own busy schedule get in the way of your foster child spending time with his family during the holidays.

> What's the point of being alive if you don't at least try to do something remarkable?
>
> — ANONYMOUS

TIP #356: If visits are not possible between your foster child and her birth family during the holiday season, try to set up phone conversations instead. As always, you will need to monitor the phone conversation for her safety. You can do this by simply placing the phone on speaker during your foster child's conversation with her family and attending to other tasks in the room.

> You can do anything, but not everything.
>
> — ANONYMOUS

TIP #357: You might want to consider having your foster child's siblings or birth parents come to your house for a holiday meal. This does not need to take place on the specific holiday. Instead, you can plan and organize a party or meal somewhere around the holiday time. If this is not possible, consider gathering at a local restaurant or park. This will both show the birth parents that you are considerate of their feelings during this time and show your foster child that he does not have to choose between you and his family.

> Instead of growing in my belly, they grew in my heart.
>
> — ANONYMOUS

TIP #358: There is sure to be some anxiety from your foster child about her birth parents and siblings during the holiday time if she is unable to visit or speak with them. She might even feel some guilt, as she is living in a comfortable, warm, and caring home while others in her family may be living in poor and unsafe conditions—or may even be homeless. Reassure her that her feelings are normal.

> You may have to fight a battle more than once to win it.
>
> —MARGARET THATCHER

TIP #359: Don't forget that traditions matter. Tell your foster child about how your family celebrates the holiday and include him in these traditions. Ask him about some of the traditions that his family had and try to include some of them into your own home during the holiday. Not only will this help him to feel more comfortable and part of your family, but it will also help to reassure him that he is important, as are his family and traditions.

> Our children need us to be with them. Not just on Christmas day, but all through the year.
>
> — JOHN DEGARMO

TIP #360: Your foster child may be worried and concerned that her birth family are not getting gifts during the holiday season. One way you can help your foster child is by allowing her to purchase gifts for her family during the holiday season. You can also help her make gifts and presents, as handmade crafts can be wonderful gifts as well. Help her design and create her own Christmas and holiday cards, as well.

> And now these three remain: faith, hope, and love. But the greatest of these is love.
>
> —1 CORINTHIANS 13:13

TIP #361: If your foster child should send cards and gifts to his biological parents and birth family during the holiday season, make sure that your return address is not on the envelope or package. This will help to protect your own family. Instead, ask your caseworker if you can use the address of their agency as a return address on the envelope or package.

> It is part of our role as a foster parent to bring a sense of self-worth back to our foster child.
>
> — JOHN DEGARMO

TIP #362: Don't ignore religious practices. Your foster child may have different religious beliefs than your family. Take time to learn about these different beliefs and practices, and if you feel comfortable, try to include some of them into your own family traditions during the holiday season—or in general.

> Parenthood requires love, not DNA.
>
> — ANONYMOUS

TIP #363: Holidays are about family. If you have been a foster parent for some time, chances are that you have had a number of children come and live in your home and become part of your family. During the holiday season, pick up the phone and call those foster children that used to live with you. Send a gift card, invite them over for a meal, or give them a wrapped gift; show them, in some way, that they are still part of your family. The holidays can be a very difficult time for those who have aged out of the foster care system.

Some people just need you to care about them.

—ANONYMOUS

TIP #364: Show your love! Your foster child needs your love. Don't be afraid to tell her that you love her each day. Don't be afraid to give her a hug each day. Tell her how important she is and that you are happy she has joined your family. Find a way to make her feel special each day.

> Today is the day that a child needs love.
>
> — JOHN DEGARMO

TIP #365: The world has not changed from you being a foster parent. What has changed is the world for the child you are caring for; you have changed your foster child's world. Your love has made a tremendous difference in his life. Years later, he will look back and remember that he was loved by you. Your love has planted a seed in him that will forever change him and blossom into something beautiful. Always remember this.

> Love your family. Spend time, be kind, and serve one another. Make no room for regrets.
>
> — ANONYMOUS

ABOUT THE AUTHOR

Dr. John DeGarmo has been a foster parent for fifteen years, and he and his wife have had over fifty-five children come through their home. DeGarmo is the founder and director of The Foster Care Institute. He is an international consultant for legal firms and foster care agencies, as well as an empowerment and transformational speaker and trainer on many topics about the foster care system. He is the author of several books and writes for several publications. Dr. DeGarmo has appeared on CNN HLN, Good Morning America, Freeform, and elsewhere. He and his wife have received many awards, including the Good Morning America Ultimate Hero Award. He can be contacted at drjohndegarmo@gmail.com; through his Facebook page, Dr. John DeGarmo; or at The Foster Care Institute.

ABOUT FAMILIUS

VISIT OUR WEBSITE: WWW.FAMILIUS.COM

Familius is a global trade publishing company that publishes books
and other content to help families be happy. We believe that the
family is the fundamental unit of society and that happy families
are the foundation of a happy life. We recognize that every family
looks different, and we passionately believe in helping all families
find greater joy. To that end, we publish books for children and adults
that invite families to live the Familius Nine Habits of Happy Family
Life: *love together*, *play together*, *learn together*, *work together*,
talk together, *heal together*, *read together*, *eat together*, and *laugh
together*. Founded in 2012, Familius is located in Sanger, California.

JOIN OUR FAMILY

There are lots of ways to connect with us! Subscribe to our news-
letters at www.familius.com to receive uplifting daily inspiration,
essays from our Pater Familius, a free ebook every month, and the
first word on special discounts and Familius news.

GET BULK DISCOUNTS

If you feel a few friends and family might benefit from what you've
read, let us know and we'll be happy to provide you with quantity
discounts. Simply email us at orders@familius.com.

CONNECT

Facebook: www.facebook.com/paterfamilius
Twitter: @familiustalk, @paterfamilius1
Pinterest: www.pinterest.com/familius
Instagram: @familiustalk

The most important work you ever do will
be within the walls of your own home.